Random Thoughts From a Disciple of Jesus Christ: Commentary on America's "Hot Button" Issues

Dr. Mike Spaulding

DEDICATION

This book is dedicated to my four beautiful daughters, Angie, Krissy, Lindsey and Sierra. God has allowed me to watch you accept Jesus Christ as your personal Lord and Savior, grow up, get married, and to have children of your own. I am honored that you call me Dad.

CONTENTS

ACKNOWLEDGMENTS

An excellent wife, who can find? For her worth is far above jewels. The heart of her husband trusts in her, and he will have no lack of gain. She does him good and not evil all the days of her life.
Proverbs 31:10-12

My dear beloved Kathy: God made you just for me. Our love can never grow old, it's evergreen. I thank our Father every day for His gift of you to me. My heart smiles every time I hear these lyrics my love:

"People fall in love in mysterious ways
Maybe just the touch of a hand
Well, me—I fall in love with you every single day…
We found love right where we are.

INTRODUCTION

American's are in near unanimous agreement that there are serious problems that need to be addressed in our nation. Disagreement exists related to what the solutions are. As a born again, spirit-filled believer in Jesus Christ, my solutions will be focused on what individual believers and collectively, what the church must do to return America to a more sure foundation for shared life together.

I believe the church has been silent for too long and much of the hatred, violence, and outright demonic manifestations we see today is the result of a silent church. What can Americans who care about this nation do? The first thing we must do is speak out. We must speak the truth in plain English. We must stop speaking in euphemisms for fear of offending. As Coach Dave Daubenmire is fond of saying, "Truth sounds like hate to those who hate the truth."

Next, we must become activists. Part of the Great Commission of Jesus is to "go and tell." Let's take that command to heart and go tell our local elected officials, our state officials, and our federal officials to start toeing the line or we will fire them. Let's do the same thing with our school boards. Then follow through on those promises.

Finally, we must stop wasting our time on apostates. Much of organized Christian religion is in full blown apostasy.

They have abandoned the faith. Jude says they are "mockers, following after their own ungodly lusts…cause divisions, (they are) worldly minded, devoid of the Spirit." (Jude 18-19)

This book is a collection of commentaries on issues we face as Americans and as the true church of the Lord Jesus Christ. I hope that you will gain courage to share these principles with your family, friends, and co-workers.

This book starts with five chapters of encouragement to remind you who we are as believers in the Lord Jesus Christ. The remainder of the book covers a wide range of issues and what we can do to address them.

Friends, those of you who belong to Christ through faith have nothing to fear from the evil doers in our midst. These people have relied on fear for too long. Let's rise up together and look them right in the eye and say, "No more. By the power and authority of Jesus Christ we rebuke you and the evil influence in you that motivates you to such hatred and destruction." Let's march together under Christ's banner.

For Christ's glory!

Mike

Chapter One

Becoming a Man of God: Lessons from the Life of David

Part 1 – Grace Given and Received

The Bible presents a picture of David that is both inspiring and perplexing. We know David as a magnificent warrior, a man of humility and integrity. We also know David as an adulterer and in the least an accomplice to murder.

In 2 Samuel 3 we read that David had multiple wives. 2 Samuel 11 contains the story of Bathsheba and Uriah her husband. In 2 Samuel 13 & 18 we see that David was a negligent father and this in turn caused much strife, heartache and even bloodshed.

Yet in speaking to Saul about David the Bible declares in 1 Samuel 13:14:

> *"But now your kingdom shall not endure. The LORD has sought out for Himself a man after His own heart, and the*

> LORD *has appointed him as ruler over His people, because you have not kept what the LORD commanded you."*

And in Acts 13:22 we read:

> *"After He had removed him, He raised up David to be their king, concerning whom He also testified and said, 'I HAVE FOUND DAVID the son of Jesse, A MAN AFTER MY HEART, who will do all My will.'*

What a statement from God! But the question remains: How could God declare David "a man after His own heart?" One of the keys to understanding this declaration is to understand that God is not looking for perfection. That is only found in the Lord Jesus Christ.

Instead God is looking for men and women upon whom He can bestow His mercy and grace. God looks for people whose hearts are pliable and seeking to serve Him. God desires to pour out upon us His loving-kindness.

In 2 Samuel 9 we see this picture clearly.

This is a time in David's life when God is very much blessing him. Militarily, he has expanded Israel's borders. 2 Samuel 8 tells us that he waged war with and conquered the Philistines, the Moabites, and the Arameans (Syrians). He established military outposts in those and other nations to secure his borders and bring peace.

Although God had already told him he would not build the Temple, he nevertheless collected precious metals, jewels, and building materials for his son Solomon who would build it.

If we were to describe this time in the life of David and in the nation of Israel we would say that "life was good" or David was "living large."

As David sat on his throne his mind began to recount God's goodness toward him. No doubt his thoughts drifted to Jonathan his best friend. I believe even the words of their covenant came back to him. 1 Samuel 20:12-16 gives us the details.

> *Then Jonathan said to David, "The LORD, the God of Israel, be witness! When I have sounded out my father about this time tomorrow, or the third day, behold, if there is good feeling toward David, shall I not then send to you and make it known to you?*
>
> *"If it please my father to do you harm, may the LORD do so to Jonathan and more also, if I do not make it known to you and send you away, that you may go in safety and may the LORD be with you as He has been with my father.*
>
> *"If I am still alive, will you not show me the loving-kindness of the LORD that I may not die?*
>
> *"You shall not cut off your loving-kindness from my house forever, not even when the LORD cuts off every one of the enemies of David from the face of the earth."*

So Jonathan made a covenant with the house of David, saying, "May the LORD require it at the hands of David's enemies."

V1 Notice that David makes his inquiry because his heart has been stirred by remembering the loving kindness he and Jonathan made a vow to uphold.

V2 Someone knew of a servant from the house of Saul whose name was Ziba. They called Ziba to come before the king and answer some questions.

V3 This son of Jonathan became crippled in his feet when his father and his grandfather King Saul were killed in a battle against the Philistines described in 2 Samuel 4. It was customary and expected that when a new king ascended the throne the former king's family would be executed. When the house of Saul heard of his death, the nurse maid for Jonathan's son scooped him in haste and attempted to escape. Unfortunately the child she held in her arms was dropped and he became crippled in both feet from the age of 5.

V4 David was overjoyed at this news and wanted to know where this son of Jonathan was. I find this interesting that this descendant had been so well hidden as to be forgotten. Remember that one of David's wives was Michal, the daughter of Saul and thus the sister of Jonathan. Even she did not know of this nephew.

V5 So David sent for this son of Jonathan to be brought to him. Can you imagine what must have been going through this young man's life when David's servants came for him? "The gigs up. I made it a few years but it's over now." No doubt this child's servants told him that his life must remain secret or else David would kill him. After all, his grandfather chased David all over the desert trying to kill him so he could expect nothing less from David.

V6 We finally hear the name of Jonathan's son. Mephibosheth – "shameful one." His name was Merib-baal at birth but perhaps was changed to Mephibosheth after he was crippled. Notice that Mephibosheth thought his life was over and so he fell on his face before David as if resigned to his fate.

V7 "Fear Not." I imagine that took several long, tense moments to sink in. Mephibosheth was there on his face before the king expecting at any moment to have his head cut off and instead he hears these beautiful words that brought indescribable joy.

V8 So Mephibosheth did the most reasonable thing – he spoke of himself as an unworthy recipient of this kindness. I think he wanted to clarify what David had said and so he referred to himself as a "dead dog." This was a Jewish idiom of the time that represented the most worthless thing one could imagine.

V9 To make it official David calls in Ziba, the servant in Mephibosheth's house to tell him that from that day forward Saul's possessions including his ancestral lands would be Mephibosheth's.

V10 Notice that along with Mephibosheth's ancestral wealth being restored he would also eat at the king's table. Eating at the king's table was an honor and represented the highest favor a king could bestow. David was in effect saying "you'll never have need of anything else again. You are now under my protection and blessing."

V11-13 David looked at Mephibosheth as one of his sons. What a great story of kindness fulfilled. It demonstrates the heart of a man of honor and integrity.

But there is so much more here that God wants us to see. Let's look again at this same text from God's perspective if we can presume to know it.

The Bible tells us that God sent His Son into the world to save the world. It is God's desire to save the people of the house of Adam, to show kindness to them for Christ's sake because of the covenant in Jesus' blood.

In this story of David and Mephibosheth we see a picture of God the Father reaching out to us with salvation in His hands. Can't you hear God asking "Isn't there one more of the line of Adam that I can show my mercy and grace to?"

Here is the first mark of the man of God – he has been born again, transformed by the Spirit of God to enter into that covenant relationship established by Jesus Christ.

In verse three Ziba the servant identifies Mephibosheth not

by his name but by his condition – "There is a son of Jonathan who is crippled in both feet."

Brothers, we should see in Mephibosheth ourselves first and then all of lost humanity. Just as Mephibosheth could not walk because of a fall, so too we are unable to seek after God because we are fallen creatures. We were all lame at one time.

It is interesting that Mephibosheth's name means shameful one. What did he do to deserve that? He was rendered lame by the actions of someone else. What a picture of the fall of Adam and the stain of sin upon all mankind.

King David, picturing God in this passage asks "where is he?" Doesn't that remind you of the Garden of Eden? God asked Adam and Eve where they were not because he did not know where they were but because he wanted them to understand the fall they had suffered because of their sin.

They thought they were hiding. They tried to cover themselves with fig leaves. But they could not hide the desolation of soul that exploded into their conscience. Sooner than later sin betrays us and we are found for who we are.

Notice in verse 4 Ziba answers the King's question of where Mephibosheth is by telling him that he is in Lo-debar. Lo-debar means place of desolation, barrenness, and unfruitfulness. That is the condition of all men apart from a saving faith in Jesus Christ. Mephibosheth had been taken there to hide from the King.

That's where I was when God called me. I was in the desert hiding from Him. Funny thing about the desert though – I didn't see it as an utterly barren place. It was only after His Holy Spirit began to work upon my soul to bring that sweet conviction to fruition that I saw the green pastures God was asking me to come lay down in.

Praise God that he did not leave us there in the desert. Verse 5 says the King sent for Mephibosheth. God calls out to men and women everywhere to come to Him. He sends His Holy Spirit to bear witness and bring conviction. He sends His servants, missionaries, pastors, Sunday School teachers, men and women of every walk of life to bear witness to His goodness.

The Bible says that Jesus came to seek and to save that which was lost. In this church age He likes to use His children.

So Mephibosheth, representative of you and I, is summoned to the King. Do you recall when you were summoned to the King? There is a conviction in our souls. We might not understand it completely but we know that God is real and He is calling out to us. What do we do? The only thing we can do, we fall face to the ground in trembling fear not knowing what to expect.

Isn't that a good picture of how most people see God? Mephibosheth was thinking the worse. He thought the King was about to whack him. When God calls us He is seeking to bless us not whack us.

Verse 7 – "Fear not." God doesn't call out to us to come to Him with fear. God wants to show us kindness because of what Jesus has already done for us. David says that his blessing to Mephibosheth will include restoring to him all that his grandfather Saul had.

In the same way God restores to us all that Adam had before his fall. What would that be?

> 1) Intimate fellowship/communion with Him. God desires that close personal relationship with His children.
>
> 2) The King invites you to dine at His table as one of His sons. The King's table is the place of abundance brothers. The King's table is a place of warmth, blessing, and joy. The King's table is a place of fellowship.
>
> 3) The King did all this for Mephibosheth not because he deserved it but solely for Jonathan's sake, because of the covenant he had made with Jonathan. We benefit by what Jesus has done for us.

This is a second mark of the man of God – fear is replaced by an understanding of the overwhelming grace God has to bestow upon us in Christ Jesus.

David wrote long before this, "He prepares a table before me in the presence of my enemies." Do you see the picture? Rest and comfort in the blessings of God replace fear even in the direst circumstances.

This is an overwhelming picture to be sure. Mephibosheth was flabbergasted. He put his face to the ground a 2nd time and declared that he was not worthy of such grand treatment. Isn't that a picture of the ones God calls to Himself?

Jesus said in Matthew 5 "blessed are the poor in spirit for theirs is the kingdom of heaven." God's invitation to us will not produce a sense of pride but will always stir within us a sense of unworthiness. That's the humility required of the man of God.

I'm reminded here of Jacob's testimony before the Lord "I am unworthy of all the loving-kindness and of all the faithfulness which You have shown to Your servant" (Gen 32:10).

Notice verse 13 – Mephibosheth ate at the King's table regularly. I love that. We may not understand why God would bless us but we can accept it and enjoy it forever! We're not to camp out on our unworthiness. That can create a false piety. Instead we are to receive the Lord's goodness toward us with joy.

What a wonderful picture for the man of God. Let me pull all this together and give you some points to chew on.

First, God desires to spend time with you. He has poured out His grace and mercy upon you in salvation but that's not the end. Consider how many times David sat alone with Mephibosheth telling him about his father, how Jonathon loved Mephibosheth, about his friendship with his father, about their covenant of trust.

God wants to sit with us and tell us "Behold, what manner of love the Father hath bestowed upon us, that we should be called the sons of God" (1 John 3:1).

The songwriter has well said:

> How deep the Father's love for us,
> How vast beyond all measure
> That He should give His only Son
> To make a wretch His treasure
>
> How great the pain of searing loss,
> The Father turns His face away
> As wounds which mar the chosen One,
> Bring many sons to glory
>
> Behold the Man upon a cross,
> My sin upon His shoulders
> Ashamed I hear my mocking voice,
> Call out among the scoffers
>
> It was my sin that held Him there
> Until it was accomplished
> His dying breath has brought me life
> I know that it is finished
>
> I will not boast in anything

No gifts, no power, no wisdom
But I will boast in Jesus Christ
His death and resurrection
Why should I gain from His reward?
I cannot give an answer
But this I know with all my heart
His wounds have paid my ransom.[1]

Second, notice that David says no less than four times in this passage that Mephibosheth will "eat at my table continually." What a wonderful picture of God's abundant grace for all we need.

Alan Redpath in his book "The Making of a Man of God" says this:

"In Christ we are more than conquerors! In Him there is a constant supply of life to the helpless and penitent sinner who has come to the foot of the cross. At Calvary he discovers real satisfaction. Instead of barrenness in his life, there is fruitfulness; instead of being far off, he is made near to God by the blood of Jesus. From that moment on, he is the object of God's outpouring of blessing. All the resources of heaven are made available to meet his need and to take him safely through the journey of life until one day he will be presented faultless at the throne of God."

[1] Stuart Townend Copyright © 1995 Thankyou Music (Adm. by CapitolCMGPublishing.com excl. UK & Europe, adm. by Integrity Music, part of the David C Cook family, songs@integritymusic.com)

Third, David's grace to Mephibosheth is a pattern for us in serving and ministering to others. In a sense David represents the man God wants us to become.

For example we can see from this passage that perhaps God is saying:

- We should look for the poor, weak, lame, and hidden to bless them.
- We should bless others even when they don't deserve it, and bless them more than they deserve.
- We should bless others for the sake of someone else.
- We should show the *kindness of God* to others.

Friends I pray you will think on these things and seek wisdom from God and understand the application of them in your own lives. May our great God bless you abundantly as you seek to honor Him in every word and deed.

Dr. Mike Spaulding

Chapter Two

Becoming a Man of God: Lessons from the Life of David

Part 2 – A Man After God's Own Heart

King David is often referred to as the "Shepherd King." He spent his adolescent and young teenage years tending his father's sheep as we will see in this study. I believe it was from that foundation of servant hood, being seen and treated as the least among his brethren that David developed into a man of integrity, honor, and humbleness.

As a king, David was no hireling. He loved the people of Israel and was a faithful shepherd to them. I recommend the book by Philip Keller, *"A Shepherd Looks at the 23rd Psalm."* Keller paints a beautiful picture in words of the life of a shepherd and the sheep he cares for.

The Bibles says that hirelings get out in front of the slowest

sheep when the wolves come. Hirelings take off and leave the sheep unprotected. David never did that. Instead he protected them against all sort of wild animals.
That reminds me of the story I heard recently about the two friends that went on an overnight camping trip to the mountains.

In the middle of the night they were both awakened by a ferocious roar of what they both knew was a grizzly bear. They both sat up in their cots frantically trying to get out of their sleeping bags and out of the tent before the bear was upon them.

In the midst of this mad scramble one guy looks at his friend and the friend is putting on his tennis shoes. The first guy half yelled "you don't have time for that and putting on your tennis shoes won't help you out run the bear."

His friend responded "I don't have to out run the bear. I only have to outrun you."

The Bible speaks more about David than any other person except Jesus Christ. Consider for example that:

- 14 chapters about Abraham, the father of the faithful.
- 14 chapters about Joseph whom God used to preserve His people.
- 13 chapters about Jacob the patriarch who wrestled with God.

- 10 chapters about Elijah the prophet who slew 400 false prophets.

But there are ~ 65 chapters of the Bible dedicated to the life of David. The NT mentions David 59 times. This affords a comprehensive view of the life of this man. I believe God holds David up as an example of "a man after His own heart" because David's heart was always seeking after Him.

I love the picture that God gives us of David – his triumphs, his victories, his greatest moments all right alongside of his failures, his defects, and his sins.

I want to look at 1 Samuel 16. Let me set the context of what we'll be studying.

The date is around 1126 BC. Israel left Egypt about 340 years before this time and thus had been in the Promised Land about 300 years. Within those 300 years was a 240 year period of time known as the "time of the judges." People such as Samson, Gideon, Deborah, Abimelech, and Jepthah had given counsel to and provided protection for God's people.

You may recall that the book of Judges closes with this statement: "In those days there was no king in Israel; everyone did what was right in his own eyes." It was at this time that God raised up Samuel the prophet who in effect became the last judge.

It was to Samuel that the Israelites came begging for a king because they wanted to be like other nations. There's a lesson there for us — it is always a sign of danger ahead when God's people decide to imitate the world.

So, Samuel eventually anoints Saul as Israel's first king. We read about that in chapters 9-10 of 1 Samuel. Saul's reign was marked by victory and defeat.

God removed the kingdom from him because he did not obey Him in all that he was instructed — first by offering strange fire before the Lord (1 Sam 13) and then by disobeying God's instructions to completely wipe out the Amalekites (1 Sam 15).

Samuel's announcement to Saul is a key to understanding the text we will consider. Samuel the prophet speaks thusly to King Saul in 1 Samuel 13:14:

> *"But now your kingdom shall not endure. The Lord has sought out for Himself a man after His own heart, and the Lord has appointed him as ruler over His people, because you have not kept what the Lord commanded you."*

1 Samuel 16:1-13

<u>V1</u> Samuel was *still* grieving. I think this is an important point being made here. Why would God include this piece of information? Saul had messed up and God rejected him.

What I see here is that the man of God grieves for God's people who have fallen into sin. There is a time to grieve for our brothers and sisters.

There should be no joy in the heart of a believer when a brother or sister falls. We may know that it was self-induced. We may have even seen it coming and tried to warn them but when it comes there should be a sense of heartache.

Notice God asks Samuel "how long" he is going to grieve. God is saying "let's get up and get back to work." That tells me that grieving should not be debilitating. It should not cause us to forget about the tasks God has called us to.

God instructs Samuel to fill his horn with oil. What a picture that is. The horn represents strength in the Bible and oil represents the Holy Spirit. God is saying to Samuel "I am sending you forth in the strength of the Holy Spirit."

It's important for us to remember that regardless of the circumstances we might find ourselves facing, God is with us and His strength is our strength. We never face our obstacles alone. When we obey God we always move forward filled with the Holy Spirit.

V2 As is often the case, we miss God's encouragement and provision. Samuel's eyes were not focusing on the Lord any longer but on the fate of Saul and the potential for Saul's anger to turn toward him.

Here's another lesson for us. When God calls us to a work

He will strengthen us for it and provide the enabling to do it. "Where God guides God provides." If we keep looking to Him for this provision we will succeed. When we take our eyes off of Him and examine our circumstances we give doubt and anxiety an open door.

I love God's response to Samuel's fear – "Here's the plan. Take a heifer with you and go make a sacrifice." God is saying "listen to Me Samuel. I've got this under control. Do as I ask."

<u>V3</u> God gives Samuel just enough information to get him to the right place in front of the right people. Do you see the important piece of information that God withholds? God did not tell Samuel to anoint the tallest or the strongest or the most handsome. God didn't give Samuel a name. He didn't ask for Samuel's opinion at all. He merely told Samuel to anoint the one that He would designate.

That took the burden off Samuel didn't it? All Samuel had to do was go to Jesse's house and wait for God to tell him which man to anoint as the next King of Israel.

We can walk with great confidence when we understand that following God's plan to the letter releases us from the burden of making sure something is successful.

When we listen to God and don't attempt to "tweak" His plans we can rest in the knowledge that whatever God chooses is the best possible choice. That's true freedom.

- So from this verse we learn that God calls people to *walk by faith*. He calls us to *trust Him with the results*.
- We can also say that God desires *constant communication* with us. He gives us enough information to take the next step in obedience to Him. That insures that we will not get too far ahead.
- That segues into a 3rd point here – God wants us to be *continually dependent upon Him*.

<u>V4</u> "So Samuel did as the Lord said." That's a great statement. After receiving instruction from God, Samuel carried those instructions out.

The elders of the city of Bethlehem were concerned because "the" prophet of God, the judge of Israel, the King's closest advisor had come to their Podunk village unannounced. That caused a near panic. We're not told why exactly. They rightly thought he was there for a specific reason.

<u>V5</u> Samuel calms their fears and invites them to the sacrifice. What he doesn't tell them is this is a sacrifice of consecration. Someone is about to be "set apart" for service to the Lord. This awareness was mysteriously lost upon them.

- Point – God will always consecrate or set apart a man for service. God has His own qualifications that look nothing like what the world thinks is important.

- I've seen a few men over the years that have claimed God told them to become a pastor. Time has demonstrated that their calling was not from God.

<u>V6-10</u> We see in these verses that God looks at the heart of a man not the outward appearance. Outward appearance means the total package of externals including our words and our actions. When the internals are not right then the externals don't matter to God.

In America we teach young people to aggressively "sell themselves." We tell them that "first impressions" are the most important. The result has been what we see today – inflated egos and inflated résumés.

God sees through all the "veneer." He doesn't need our talents, abilities, or experiences in order to accomplish His plans through us. All He needs is a man with a right heart.

Alan Redpath said "Jesse's seven sons represented the perfection of the flesh. Outwardly they fit the criteria but God is no interested in refining the flesh. When God chooses to build a man He looks for different timber."

So the man of God understands that *the basis for God's choice is contrary to human reasoning.* This in turn will deliver us from the tyranny of judging people without knowing the heart. I have shared my testimony before and a part of that testimony is that I can't believe that God chose me to be one of His.

Perhaps that is your testimony too. God's grace toward us is not an occasion for boasting or haughtiness. Instead experiencing God's love toward us should cause us to be humble.

- Paul in writing to the Corinthian believers said: "What do you have that you did not receive? And if you did receive it, why do you boast as if you had not received it?" (1 Cor. 4:7)

We should remember that when it comes to sharing our faith and living for Christ. We don't know who God is going to call into His Kingdom nor should we care. God will call whom He will call. Our job is be ready "in season and out of season" to share a word of encouragement when the opportunity presents itself.

I see those points being made next – V11-13

I think God delights in choosing those the world least expects. Paul said exactly that in 1 Corinthians 1:

"Because the foolishness of God is wiser than men, and the weakness of God is stronger than men. For consider your calling, brethren, that there were not many wise according to the flesh, not many mighty, not many noble; but God has chosen the foolish things of the world to shame the wise, and God has chosen the weak things of the world to shame the things which are strong, and the base things of the world and the despised God has chosen, the things that are not, so that He may nullify the things that are, so that no man may boast before God" (v25-29).

Why does God do that? Well I don't pretend to know the mind of God but I will say that I believe one reason God chooses the least expected option is because that way He gets all the glory. It's easy to give God the glory when great things are accomplished through ordinary people.

We can look to our own heritage as Calvary Chapel and know this is true. Pastor Chuck in obedience agreed to pastor a little church called Calvary Chapel that boasted a congregation of 25 people.

Most people don't know that Bob Coy was the "go to" guy for making sure rock stars in Detroit had a good time. Most people don't know that Greg Laurie was a drug dealer and user or that Mike Macintosh was so strung out on drugs at one point he didn't think he would survive mentally.

I look at an uneducated shoe salesman like DL Moody and think wow! Who had ever heard of Billy Graham? He didn't come up through the right seminary and church group. All of these men have one thing in common – they had a right heart before God.

This was God's testimony about David. He was a man "after" God's own heart. I think this means David longed to be near God and to hear from Him.

As the deer pants for the water brooks, so my soul pants for You, O God. My soul thirsts for God, for the living God; When shall I come and appear before God? (Ps 42:1-2)

One thing I have asked from the LORD, that I shall seek: That I may dwell in the house of the LORD all the days of my life, to behold the beauty of the LORD and to meditate in His temple. (Ps 27:4)

One of the things that I want you to take away from this passage is that David is not the exception. I don't want you to look at his life and say "yea but . . ." David's life is presented to us in Scripture as a model of what can be for every man of God.

- *"For the eyes of the LORD move to and fro throughout the earth that He may strongly support those whose heart is completely His" (2 Chronicles 16:9)*

God is looking for men whose hearts are completely His. There's nothing hidden or being held onto; nothing being swept under the rug, nothing being ignored.

So God is holding up David as an example to us and says "learn from this picture. Be a man whose supreme desire is to know Me and to be known by Me."

David's heart was in-tune with God and because of that he could cry even in the most burdensome times "create in me a clean heart oh God." Oh for a walk like that.

What will that take on our part? I will take at least two things.

1) We must learn to see as God sees. This will require us to spend much more time on the preparation of our hearts for God than it does on the preparation of our outward appearance. This will require us to work on the "issues" of the heart continually, to bring our thoughts and our wills into conformity to His.

2) We must learn to constantly check our priorities. What am I spending the most time on? What do I spend the least time on? Are there things that I should move up the list or down the list?

Chapter Three

Becoming a Man of God: Lessons from the Life of David

Part 3 – A Heart Prepared For Worship

I conclude this three part teaching on becoming a man of God by focusing on the glory of God. By that I mean the presence of God in our lives. What will it take to have the glory of God manifested in our lives? How do we live in such a way that God's presence is near?

Our text for this segment involves King David seeking to bring the Ark of the Covenant to Jerusalem. Having consolidated his political power in the Holy City, David then moved to make Jerusalem the religious center as well.

He wants to place the Ark in the Tabernacle he has built and subsequently in a Temple for God he hopes to build. We know that God did not allow David to build the Temple. That honor went to David's son Solomon.

In a sense mankind is pictured in this episode. Man has been created to know the reality of God and to long for

His presence. There is emptiness within man that can only be filled by the presence of God.

The Hebrew for glory is "kabod." The word carries the idea of substance, depth, and weightiness within a context of significance and worth. I think this is the reason people ask questions such as, "Why am I here?" "What is my life about?" or "Where is my life heading and why?" These are all questions related to significance.

It's very interesting that once a person is born-again those questions become focused on God's presence. "How can I draw nearer to God?" "How can I experience more of God in my life?" "God, what is your plan for my life?" These questions relate to God's significance to us.

Let's examine a passage of scripture this morning that presents a beautiful picture of the way to experience the glory and presence of God. I've entitled this message "A Heart Prepared For Worship."

2 Samuel 6:1-23

V1-2 The Ark of the Covenant was the central fixture in the worship of Israel. It was placed in the Holy of Holies and was where God's presence dwelled with the nation. The OT refers to it as the "Shekinah Glory." You may recall that the Ark held the 10 Commandments, Aaron's rod, and manna that fed the Hebrew people in their desert wanderings.

The Ark was the place where the priest would take a goat one day a year – The Day of Atonement – and sacrifice it there for the sins of the Hebrew people.

Kiriath-jearim (Joshua 15:9) was the ancient name of Baale-judah. This village was about 9 miles from Jerusalem.

David called together 30,000 Israelites to help him celebrate bringing the Ark to Jerusalem. At the heart of the issue for David was a longing for the presence of God in his life and in the national life of Israel. He understood the need to be close to God and it was his heart's desire to experience that closeness.

We see that in many of the Psalms David wrote. Psalm 63 for example says:

> *O God, You are my God; I shall seek You earnestly; My soul thirsts for You, my flesh yearns for You, in a dry and weary land where there is no water. Thus I have seen You in the sanctuary, to see Your power and Your glory. Because Your lovingkindness is better than life, my lips will praise You. So I will bless You as long as I live; I will lift up my hands in Your name. My soul is satisfied as with marrow and fatness, and my mouth offers praises with joyful lips. When I remember You on my bed, I meditate on You in the night watches, for You have been my help, and in the shadow of Your wings I sing for joy. My soul clings to You; Your right hand upholds me (v. 1-8).*

In Psalm 84 David proclaims:

> *How lovely are Your dwelling places, O LORD of hosts! My*
> *soul longed and even yearned for the courts of the LORD;*
> *My heart and my flesh sing for joy to the living God. O*
> *LORD God of hosts, hear my prayer; Give ear, O God of*
> *Jacob! Selah.*
> *Behold our shield, O God, and look upon the face of Your*
> *anointed. For a day in Your courts is better than a thousand*
> *outside. I would rather stand at the threshold of the house of*
> *my God than dwell in the tents of wickedness. For the*
> *LORD God is a sun and shield;*
> *The LORD gives grace and glory; No good thing does He*
> *withhold from those who walk uprightly. O LORD of hosts,*
> *how blessed is the man who trusts in You! (v.1-2, 8-12)*

V3-5 The Ark was loaded onto a new cart. This fact is presented because the Philistines sent the Ark back to the Hebrews on a cart. So the Israelites built a new cart for the Ark and did not us the same cart.

This was a time of celebration and must have been a grand parade. With 30,000 people playing instruments, shouting, and dancing it must have been quite a spectacle to behold.

V6-11 Along the way the oxen evidently hit a rut and the Ark slid across the cart bed and looked as if it was going to tip over. Instinctively, Uzzah, one of Abinadab's sons put his hand out to stop the Ark from falling off the cart.

Can you image the pall that fell upon the people? Get the picture – the people in front of the cart would not have known about God striking Uzzah dead but the people following the cart would have seen it. As Uzzah fell to the ground dead all dancing, shouting, and instruments would have fallen into stunned silence.

The cart would have been stopped and slowly one by one the celebrants in front would realize something had gone terribly wrong. As word spread throughout the crowd all the way to King David, a hushed murmur would have risen as David walked back to the lifeless body of Uzzah.

Notice David's response. First anger, then fear, then a decision to abandon the Ark to the household of Obed-edom the Gittite where we are told it stayed for at least 3 months while David returned to Jerusalem with all the people. That must have been a painfully quiet return to the capital city.

In verse 9 notice the question that David asks perhaps out loud "How can the Ark of the Lord come to me?" That's a key question in this passage that we'll answer in a moment.

V12-15 When we read this account we ask what is different from the previous account of David bringing the Ark to Jerusalem. We notice that they stopped every 6 paces and sacrificed. Something else had happened though.

While the Ark was in the house of Obed-edom David returned to Jerusalem and sought an answer to the question he asked in verse 9 – how could he bring the Ark to

Jerusalem. We find the answer to that question in 1 Chronicles 15:1-2, 11-15.

1Now David built houses for himself in the city of David; and he prepared a place for the ark of God and pitched a tent for it.

2Then David said, "No one is to carry the ark of God but the Levites; for the LORD chose them to carry the ark of God and to minister to Him forever."

11Then David called for Zadok and Abiathar the priests, and for the Levites, for Uriel, Asaiah, Joel, Shemaiah, Eliel and Amminadab,

12and said to them, "You are the heads of the fathers' households of the Levites; consecrate yourselves both you and your relatives, that you may bring up the ark of the LORD God of Israel to the place that I have prepared for it.

13"Because you did not carry it at the first, the LORD our God made an outburst on us, for we did not seek Him according to the ordinance."

14So the priests and the Levites consecrated themselves to bring up the ark of the LORD God of Israel.

15The sons of the Levites carried the ark of God on their shoulders with the poles thereon, as Moses had commanded according to the word of the LORD.

This passage recounts for us that David researched the Ark and how it was to be transported. This led him to read

Exodus 25 where the specific instructions for transporting the Ark are found.

V16-23 Michal was David's first wife given to him by King Saul as a gesture of goodwill for David's heroic military conquests. When God removed His blessing and anointing from Saul one of the first things he did was give Michal to another man as a wife. She obviously believed her husband acted inappropriately before the "common people."

What does this chapter, this singular event in the life of David have to tell us? What can we take away from this that will help us in our personal lives and in our responsibilities to our families and our church? More importantly what is this story telling us about the heart of a person who worships God?

The first thing we can say is that the person who worships God must have a passion for His presence. David's heart was aflame with a desire to have God's presence near. This is what motivated him to go get the Ark in the first place.

But here lies our first warning as well. It is not enough to have the right motivation. David certainly had the right motivation. Our motivation must be coupled with a right method. This is where David went wrong.

David neglected the Word of God that gave specific instructions on how the Ark was to be transported. Notice that the Israelites built a brand new cart to haul the Ark. Why did they do that?

Partly because none of the priests knew God's Word enough to say "hey wait a minute David. God says only the Levites are to transport the Ark and they must bear the burden on poles. It cannot be touched."

The other reason is that they were quick to mimic what the Philistines had done. This enemy of the Israelites had sent the Ark away from them on a cart and thus the Hebrew people didn't think a thing about utilizing the same method.

Brethren, the cart in this chapter represents the world's ways. David was guilty of copying the world in approaching God. We must understand that God is not impressed with our good motives fulfilled in the wrong ways.

The old adage is right – the road to hell is paved with good intentions.

Notice the results in V6-11 of doing things the world's way. When we do things the world's way there will be death. People will be hurt. If we want God's presence we must do things God's way. If we want God's blessings then we must join together our right motives with God's prescribed method of approaching Him.

Some people read this account of Uzzah's death and say that God is unfair or that He is unduly harsh. They rationalize that Uzzah was trying to do a good thing. He was trying to help God by preventing the Ark from falling to the ground.

The problem with that thinking is that people overlook a fundamental truth – God doesn't need our help. How often do we think that we need to reach out our hands to steady a "work of God?" How often are we tempted to lend a hand to God because His glory and honor are slipping or falling in the world's eyes?

Notice a 2nd result of seeking God's presence using the world's methods – it results in anger and bitterness toward the Lord. David was one of those people who thought God was totally unfair to do what He did. This wrong attitude in turn led to fear.

David became afraid of the presence of God. What started out as a good thing – desiring the presence of God and setting in motion plans to accomplish that, turned into a disaster which in turn led David away from the God he longed to be near.

I see a very vivid picture of the church in this section of David's story. The church says that they desire the presence of God more than anything (Well, some churches say that).

The motives may be right – desiring the presence of God – but the method is terribly wrong. So many churches today employee Madison Avenue marketing techniques that is completely foreign to God's Word.

Many churches today look at people as consumers. So the goal for many churches today is to satisfy their customers. Churches conduct polls and surveys asking lost people what it would take to get them to come to church. Once the data is analyzed the church morphs into whatever the survey says.

People today are looking for entertainment in a church so the pastor becomes a comedian and the service becomes a fast moving collage of drama, songs, skits, and sermonettes all designed to satisfy the pew consumer.

When numbers become the goal God is not glorified. David assembled 30,000 worshippers and they were all shouting and singing and playing instruments but notice that God was not being glorified because He was not being worshipped the right way and so disaster struck. It was a great religious show but it was void of God.

Here it was physical death. Today it is spiritual death. People are coming and going through the doors of our churches dead spiritually because they are not hearing the life changing Word of God. People cannot be saved by meeting their felt needs. Salvation comes through recognition that we are sinners saved by grace.

I remember John Courson talking about this church growth/marketing phenomenon. He spoke about a group of churches uniting in a campaign to reach their city. So they got a steering team together. Sort of an ad hock board.

This board was comprised of some movers and shakers in the community. They decided that what they needed was a big wheel, a name, or several names to come into town and show folks how cool it was to be a Christian. The implication was of course that anyone could be as successful as they if they would become a Christian.

Courson concluded his story with this comment – "boards and big wheels. That's a perfect description of a cart."

Brothers, God will not bless our carts. He will not bless our slick programs, our techniques and methods that we've co-opted from the world.

You know the Levites carried the Ark of the Covenant around the Sinai desert for nearly 38 years and never stumbled. They carried the Ark through dry river beds over rocky terrain and never stumbled. The Levites carried the Ark around the city of Jericho for seven days and never once stumbled.

God didn't need a cart then and He doesn't need one now. God says to His people – you carry Me. You shoulder Me in your hearts and you carry Me everywhere you go.

In verse 13 we see a picture of David's right understanding of the holiness of God. I've already mentioned that Kiriath-jearim was 9 miles from Jerusalem. Can you imagine how long it would take you to walk 9 miles if you stopped every 6 steps and offered a sacrifice?

Why did he do this? A few answers have been offered but I believe that the literal and symbolic meet here to provide us an answer. The number 6 is the number of man in Scripture. I think David was proclaiming before God symbolically and literally that man alone cannot come before a holy God. It is only through the blood.

In order for mankind to be reconciled to God we must approach Him in the prescribed manner – through the blood of Jesus Christ.

In verse 14 we read that David danced before the Lord with all his might wearing a linen ephod. What is that telling us? It means that David gave all to God and that he did so as a man not as a King.

The same must be true of us. We do not approach God on our own merits. We might be a business owner, a wealthy merchant, an important political figure. God says that we will take off those robes of importance and approach Him as every other person.

We can understand "dancing with all our might" within a context of diligence.

> Hebrews 11:6 says, *"He is a rewarder of those who diligently seek Him."*
>
> Jeremiah 29:13: *"And you will seek Me and find Me, when you search for Me with all your heart."*
>
> Proverbs 8:17: *"I love those who love Me and those who seek Me diligently will find Me."*
>
> Proverbs 13:4: *"The soul of a lazy man desires and has nothing; but the soul of the diligent shall be made rich."*

One last item I want you to see in this passage. Verse 20 tells us of Michal's disgust with her husband. This pictures for us the truth that even though we may diligently seek God's presence and His glory in our lives there will be those who stand in opposition.

See how this develops. David is "jazzed." He has glorified God and experienced His presence by bringing the Ark to Jerusalem. He has blessed the people and sent them home to celebrate. Now he comes to his own home wanting to bless his family and gets a bucket of cold water on the head.

There will always be someone who says "don't get too crazy or wrapped up in the God thing." They might tell you "it's ok to go to church on Sunday but do you have to read your Bible all the time and pray every day?"

You keep on trucking brethren. Notice the outcome of all those who attempt to sidetrack those who desire to diligently seek the Lord's glory – verse 23 – they will be barren. Misery loves company as they say and those who are spiritually empty cannot stand being in the presence of those who are spiritually full.

Let me share this real story with you. In his book, *The Unquenchable Worshiper* Matt Redman, who has wrote so many wonderful praise and worship songs, tells the story of how he came to write the song, "The Heart of Worship."

The church Matt attended had been incredibly blessed w/some fantastic musicians & composers. The worship was incredible. But after a time, something went missing. As the bands became more proficient & the sound improved the sense of God's presence diminished.

In Matt's words, "The fire that used to characterize our worship had somehow grown cold." Where once people would enter in no matter what, we'd now wait to see what the band was like first, how good the sound was, or whether we were 'into' the songs chosen."

The pastor, Mike Pilavachi, decided to take some radical steps to turn things around. So one Sunday when the congregation arrived, they discovered the sound system had been removed & there was no one to lead worship.

Mike said, "When you come through the doors of the church on Sunday, what are you bringing as your offering to God? What are you going to sacrifice today?"

The first few meetings after that were awkward as people struggled to learn that true worship means offering one's heart to God. Giving expression to that was difficult at first, but over several weeks, people realized worship is about more than singing songs.

It didn't take long before the power & presence of God was renewed as they gathered to worship.

Over the next weeks they added the instruments back in. Matt shares, "Out of this season, I reflected on where we had come to as a church & wrote this song,"

> *When the music fades, All is stripped away, & I simply come;*
> *Longing just to bring something that's of worth That will bless Your heart.*
> *I'll bring You more than a song, For a song in itself Is not what You have required.*
> *You search much deeper within Through the way things appear; You're looking into my heart.*
> *I'm coming back to the heart of worship, & it's all about You, All about You, Jesus.*

I'm sorry, Lord, for the thing I've made it, When it's all about You, All about You, Jesus.

Brethren there is one thing God desires for us to carry into this world. It is not our fancy clothes, fancy houses, or expensive cars.

It is a changed life by the power of the Holy Spirit. It is a testimony about the goodness of God verified by a heart that seeks Him above all else. That is the Gospel message of salvation in His Son that is written on our hearts.

When we seek God's presence in our lives and are diligent to live for his glory then His joy and enabling power to live for him comes washing through our souls like a refreshing river. That is my prayer for you my readers.

As we walk this journey together may we be an encouragement to one another in godly living.

Chapter Four

The Importance of Being the Church

"And this I pray, that your love may abound still more and more in real knowledge and all discernment, so that you may approve the things that are excellent, in order to be sincere and blameless until the day of Christ; having been filled with the fruit of righteousness which comes through Jesus Christ, to the glory and praise of God."
Philippians 1:9-11

One of the most blessed things Christians are privileged to participate in is the life of a local assembly of believers. It might surprise readers to learn that the Bible in both Testaments speaks almost exclusively within the context of local bodies. The Old Testament speaks specifically about the nation, tribes, and families of the Hebrew people. Their story of failure and success in being obedient to God and in becoming the people He desired them to be is a primary storyline of the Old Testament. The New Testament reads like a manual for righteous living within the context of the local church family.

Think about this friends – Matthew wrote for a Jewish audience, Mark a Gentile audience, Luke for the benefit of Theophilus, John to Christians generally speaking, Paul to the churches in Rome, Corinth, Galatia, Ephesus, Philippi, and Colossae to name a few. One thing these letters have in common with the possible exception of Luke is that they were written to churches. One could argue that Paul's letters to Timothy were written to an individual believer but even then Paul was instructing Timothy on how to handle issues within the body of believers.

My experience has been that most modern day Christians have not considered these truths. If they did, the number of people who deprecate the church would not be so high and alarming. I've seen many developments during my walk with Jesus Christ but none quite as surprising as the great number of people who have become indifferent to the local bodies of Christ. Researchers have a name for these people. They are called the "dones." The name derives from the common attitude expressed by this demographic that they are "done" with the church, as if simply walking away from the local body is an answer to their frustration and is always a God-led decision.

Let me begin by admitting along with all those that have had a negative experience with a church, that the church has a lot of "warts." What I mean by that is that the church has a lot of blemishes. The reason is simple. Churches are comprised of people and people make messes. There are plenty of things that people rightly point to and say, "See that's the reason I don't belong to a church." Whatever your beef with the church is I'm sure you feel justified in remaining in that mindset. There are a couple of issues you need to consider if that is you though. One is that your perspective on the church is not shared by Jesus Christ. Jesus gave His life for His bride the church (Ephesians 5:23, 25). You are at odds with Jesus if you think the church is not worthy of your presence. Plainly stated friends, Jesus views His bride a lot differently than you do.

Additionally, your "feelings" shouldn't be the determining factor in whether or not you are part of a local body of believers. Feelings are a horrible barometer of truth. Knowledge should be the primary consideration. Let me illustrate. How many people have ever had doubts about their salvation? The answer is lots of people struggle with "feeling" saved. The real question you should ask yourself is this: Do you know that you are saved? Have you made a profession of faith in the finished work of Jesus Christ on Calvary's Cross to pay the penalty that sin demands? Do you know that those who are saved are a royal priesthood, a holy nation, a people for God's own possession (1 Peter 2:9)? Do you understand that Christ is building up His body by removing the impurities in us all (malice, guile, hypocrisy, envy, slander – 1 Peter 2:1)? Do you also understand that as those impurities are removed we are made a stronger "spiritual house" together (1 Peter 2:5)? Being a part of the body means going through life together, sharing one another's burdens, laughing and crying together, struggling to right wrongs together, and sharpening each other's thinking on subjects of great importance to every believer today.

Being a part of a local body of believers is a birthright (John 1:12-13) that too many Christians have sold for a bowl of slop just like Esau sold his birthright. Only after Esau had flippantly given up his blessing did he realize what a huge mistake he had made. Unfortunately for him and his posterity, this one decision set his life on a course of judgment and sorrow. He lived his life for himself and for his own satisfaction and paid a steep price. His children and children's children suffered greatly for Esau's wrong thinking.

When I speak with people who have hardened their hearts against the church I often hear in their words the hissing of our enemy who says to people, "You don't need to fellowship with your brothers and sisters. You can do this alone. Remember how hurtful they have been? Who needs that?" Friends, in the end times days we live in the enemy's strategy is clearer than it has ever been – divide and conquer.

It still surprises me that some Christians trot out the worn out excuse that, "I don't have to go to church to be a Christian." No one is saying that going to church makes anyone a Christian. What people who use this excuse are often trying to say is they can be spiritual without the local body. But being spiritual is not what we are to pursue is it? Christians are called to pursue godliness not adopt some form of spirituality as a mind salve.

God has determined that the best possible context for His people to grow in grace and knowledge of Him is the local church. That is the thrust of Acts 2:41-42 which is the passage dealing with the beginning of the church at Pentecost. We read in verse 41 that three-thousand people were "added." The question is what were they added to? Clearly the local body of believers in the Lord Jesus Christ is in view. In verse 42 we find a great outline for what the church should look like even today. Note that this group of believers banded together to receive the apostle's teaching (which was Jesus' teaching – Matthew 28:19-20), to share their lives with one another (fellowship), to celebrating Christ's death on their behalf (the breaking of bread here can be understood as sharing meals together but it is more likely a reference to the Lord's Table or Communion which was still very fresh on the apostle's minds. See 1 Corinthians 11:26), and to prayer. That is a very good foundation for any local body.

Without the local body of believers, Paul's discussion of every believer having a gift that he or she should exercise for the benefit of other believers makes no sense at all. Who cares if someone has the gift of prophecy if that person never leaves his or her living room to share it with an assembled group of believers that recognize themselves as the body of Christ?

Now don't mishear me brothers and sisters. You can have a local body of believers meeting in someone's home.

That's how the first church plant I was involved in started. But at some point as you grow and more families join you it becomes impossible to continue in that setting. You will need a larger meeting place with rooms for children and a nursery and bathroom facilities. Sounds like a building that people use for their weekly gatherings to me.

Another feature that I have noticed over the years that is emblematic of the "dones" is that they become in many cases narrowly focused on a doctrine or two and those specific doctrines become their litmus test for association. There is an easy explanation for this. In a home church setting there is almost always a type "A" personality who sets the course of study and teaching and who functions for better or worse as an elder or pastor. His views on the Bible, on what are important and what isn't, and on a number of other things become the de facto home church by-laws and guidelines. Step outside of the home church leader's perspective and you'll find yourself alienated. In many cases this same doctrine or "pet tradition" was at the center of controversy and served as the reason why an individual left a church in the first place. This raises an interesting question. Who is there to keep that home church leader in check? Who is there to say, "Wait that doctrine does not line up with the Bible"? The answer is no one. There is as the Bible says wisdom in a multitude of counselors.

In addition to receiving a word of encouragement, equipping, and sometimes correction through a carefully developed teaching sermon by Holy Spirit filled and led elders, believers also need to understand that our lives in Christ are shaped together by worship through singing, by our interactions with other believers as often as we meet together, by our service to one another when needs arise, by our receiving from the Lord's Table, and by our common submission to the Word of God. These activities are nowhere encouraged nor pictured to be participated in isolation from one another. It is simply an untruth that some believers convince themselves is biblical.

Friends, the body of Christ is a multifaceted organism that grows and changes by nature. That is because the body of Christ is comprised of many different people with different perspectives on a host of topics. By standing together over time, we are made sure in the things we believe and why we believe them. A healthy body will have much discussion and debate over the years. But therein lays a secret to the church's longevity. Doctrine focuses ministry and ministry develops servant-hood. All who claim Christ by faith are to be disciples and are to make disciples and the best way to fulfill this commission is to be an active part of a local body of believers.

Another passage from Paul's letter to the Philippians is a good place to close this exhortation. In 1:27 Paul offers some words of encouragement to the believers in Philippi. He says to them, "conduct yourselves in a manner worthy of the gospel of Christ;…standing firm in one spirit, with one mind, striving together for the faith of the gospel;" and then in 2:2 he says essentially the same thing, "make my joy complete by being of the same mind, maintaining the same love, united in spirit, intent on one purpose." And then Paul identifies the foundation for being of one mind and one spirit in 2:3-4 - "Do nothing from selfishness or empty conceit, but with humility of mind regard one another as more important than yourselves; do not merely look out for your own personal interests, but also for the interests of others."

Folks, Paul is speaking about body life here. The context of the writing of the overwhelming majority of the New Testament is the local church. We learn how to be humble when we serve other people. We learn how to be untied in spirit as we grapple daily with the short comings of others as well as our own. Conceit, pride, selfishness, and ego are chipped away piece by piece all within the context of the local body of Christ as we travel this faith road together.

My encouragement to you dear reader, especially those who may have given up on the local church is to prayerfully reconsider your stance. Please seek out a local body of believers and ask God to lead you in that effort. I believe that as you pray for God to lead you, He will do exactly that; to a group of believers who have been praying for God to bring you and your family.

Chapter Five

The Importance of Having the Mind of Christ

I have found the book of Psalms to be a gold mine of knowledge and encouragement and if grasped and applied, wisdom. As most of you who follow my blog (www.drmikespaulding.com) and teaching ministry (www.thetransformingword.com) know, I have been teaching through Psalms for nearly four years now. The Bible is so full of nourishment for believers that it is a shame so many Bible teachers hurry through it as if they have a schedule to maintain. In doing so, they miss the rich texture and multi-layered significance of the Word.

One such example is what I realized recently as I studied Psalm 39 in preparation for teaching through it. The musings of David about his life and his circumstances led him to consider that perhaps his viewpoint was not accurate and so he cried out to God for a fresh perspective (verse 5).

Have you ever considered the importance of a proper perspective? The New Testament teaches that we are to be diligent in our study of the Bible so that we are able to accurately handle the "word of truth" (2 Timothy 2:15). The Apostle Paul also instructed the Corinthian believers with these words: "Brethren, do not be children in your thinking; yet in evil be infants, but in your thinking be mature" (1 Corinthians 14:20). Earlier in the same letter Paul told these believers that everyone who is born again has "the mind of Christ" (1 Corinthians 2:16). Considering that gave me pause.

What are the implications of this truth? Because we have the mind of Christ in fact and in promise, we must make the most of that; to see the world as God sees it; to think through the challenges we face today with a fresh perspective - with the mind of Christ. I found this quote from TM Moore in my digital library that captures the essence of the point I am making here.

> The mind is, together with the heart and the conscience, one of the components of the soul. It's the aspect that manages our thought processes. Those who have come to know Jesus Christ as Lord and King have been renewed in their minds; they must no longer use their brains like unbelievers do, but, instead, work to think like Jesus about everything (Eph. 4:17-24). We cannot live the full and abundant life in Christ without increasing

engagement of the mind and all its functions. To the mind falls the task of gathering, comparing, sorting, and storing all the information that comes our way. The mind creates new ideas out of fragments of thought. With our minds we formulate plans, organize our work, direct our speech, and routinely assess our progress in every facet of life. The process of thinking includes the varied activities of observing, analyzing, comparing, combining, revising, refining, improving, cataloguing, and organizing everything we think, say, and do. Further, our minds are continuously active. They pursue their God-given functions no matter what. If we're not diligently and faithfully attending to those functions, the world spirit of the age will obligingly squeeze our thinking into its own mold (Rom. 12:1, 2 Phillips version). As John Stott indicated in a book by this title, your mind matters, and it matters very much. It is indeed a terrible gift to waste, and, if we find that we're acting like children in our thinking, as the Corinthians were, then we need to press on to maturity and make the most of this glorious gift of God.

We see David doing that in Psalm 39:3 - "while I was musing the fire burned." While he was contemplating life, his life and his circumstances, his whole being burned to know, to understand, and so he cried out to God in verse 4. There David is asking God for and thanking Him for perspective. David is saying, "Help me to see life, to see myself through Your eyes God."

A proper perspective is a liberating thing to acquire. Often our perspective is flawed and it becomes a prison of the mind that is nearly impossible to escape. But for those who will seek God for His perspective there are a multitude of blessings.

Consider these three blessings of a proper God-given view of life.

(1) When we see things as God sees them we love Him more. Study carefully what the Apostle Paul wrote to the Ephesians in 3:13-21. Of particular interest is verse 13 where Paul says don't focus on my circumstances because you will despair. In other words don't lock into an earth-bound perspective. Then note verses 16-19 where Paul says instead of focusing on troubles focus on the riches you have in Christ and the great love that God has for you because when you do that you will be "filled up to all the fullness of God" (verse 19). All I can say is wow!

(2) When we gain God's perspective we see temptations as they really are and are strengthened to resist them. That is one truth we see emerging from Psalm 39:3-4. David contemplates, he "muses" about life and its ups and downs and concludes that if he is to resist the wicked (Psalm 39:2)

and if he is to resist sin and temptation (Psalm 39:1) he must acquire the mind of God (Psalm 39:4).

(3) Having God's perspective on life and circumstances protects us from being carried about by every wind and wave of false doctrine. Ephesians 4:11-16 speaks of this. Note in that passage verse 15 which says that believers are to "grow up in all aspects into Him who is the head, even Christ." We are to acquire the mind of Christ increasingly. This is the essence of spiritual maturity.

Remember friends, *"God has not given us a spirit of fear; but of power, and of love, and of a sound mind"* (2 Timothy 1:7).

Chapter Six

They Can't ALL Be True

A very common bumper sticker is making the rounds these days. This bumper sticker contains one word – COEXIST. Each letter of the word coexist utilizes a different religious symbol to spell out the word. For example in some renditions the C is a crescent moon representing Islam and the T is a cross that represents Christianity. Other religions such as Hinduism, Judaism, and Taoism are also represented. The meaning is clear – all religions must coexist if there is to be world peace.

This idea is not new. There has been an ongoing effort for decades to find common ground among the world's largest religious groups. What is new however is that the effort is now being publically advocated by the United Nations as well as several so-called "World Congresses" that meet yearly or bi-annually to discuss strategies to unite the religions of the world into one homogenous whole.

The first issue that I have with this thinking is that it is illogical and demonstrably false. The idea that all religious people must learn to coexist for peace to occur assumes that religious people are responsible for conditions other than peace. While it is a common refrain of the easily duped, the idea that religion has caused the most death and war is easily refuted.

Joseph Stalin of Russia and Mao se-Tung of China are responsible for nearly 50 million deaths of their own citizens. We don't even need to take into consideration other despots, tyrants, and dictators throughout history that easily dwarf any deaths caused by religious fanatics.

A second issue that the COEXIST mentality overlooks is this - How do you convince people who believe in diametrically opposite religious principles to forsake those? The clear answer is by coercion. That means that if the current trend of COEXIST manipulation continues you can expect to see various attempts to pass laws that drastically curtail religious expression. We are seeing this strategy being employed today in America, aimed specifically at Christianity.

A third issue with the misguided COEXIST philosophy is that advocates believe that the creation of a religious utopia will result in a global political utopia. Again, the primary cause of wars, crime, and evil generally speaking is not religion. It is the unregenerate heart of sinful man that refuses to acknowledge the Creator.

Finally, the thinking that supports a COEXIST theology ignores the impossibility of the task. In order for all religions to coexist peacefully, the primary points of difference will need to be removed completely. No other religious system teaches a personal God who came to earth and died for the sins of mankind. For Christians this means that the teaching that there is salvation in no other name but Jesus Christ will need to be denied. That is the definition of apostasy and will never happen for true believers.

Friends, do not buy into the dream of the religious utopians. That path leads to death. Stand firm in the Lord Jesus Christ and continue to proclaim the good news of salvation in Him alone. That is a transforming truth.

Chapter Seven

Who Made Your Glasses?

Buy truth, and do not sell it. Get wisdom and instruction and understanding. Proverbs 23:23

My wife Kathy and I recently met a woman and her fifteen year-old son at a conference we attended. We had the privilege of praying with and for them both. One of the things this woman shared with us was the deteriorating vision of her son who was wearing glasses. She stated that until recently her son had 20/20 vision.

I recall that meeting now within the context of the ability to see clearly as it relates to spiritual things. The Bible has much to say about seeing things accurately, as well as having spiritual insight and vision.

Consider these examples:

- *"Where there is no vision the people perish."* Proverbs 29:18

- *"So give Your servant an understanding heart to judge Your people to discern between good and evil."* **1** Kings 3:9

- *"Give me understanding, that I may observe Your law and keep it with all my heart."* Psalm 119:34

- *"For if you cry for discernment, lift your voice for understanding."* Proverbs 2:3

- *"Those who have insight will shine brightly like the brightness of the expanse of heaven, and those who lead the many to righteousness, like the stars forever and ever."* Daniel 12:3

One simple truth found throughout the Bible is that God requires His people to gain understanding of who He is, what He is doing in their lives and in the world around them, and act upon that acquired knowledge. Proverbs 23:23 supports this and says: *"Buy truth, and do not sell it. Get wisdom and instruction and understanding."*

We are instructed to seek truth and hold on to it steadfastly. We are encouraged to acquire wisdom through understanding that comes from instruction. God desires His people to become educated in spiritual matters as they pertain to Him and living for Him in righteousness and holiness day by day.

The Apostle Peter captures the essence of what it means to be a believer in the Lord Jesus Christ when he wrote these words in his second epistle:

Simon Peter, a bond-servant and apostle of Jesus Christ, to those who have received a faith of the same kind as ours, by the righteousness of our God and Savior, Jesus Christ: ² Grace and peace be multiplied to you in the knowledge of God and of Jesus our Lord; ³ seeing that His divine power has granted to us everything pertaining to life and godliness, through the true knowledge of Him who called us by His own glory and excellence. ⁴ For by these He has granted to us His precious and magnificent promises, so that by them you may become partakers of the divine nature, having escaped the corruption that is in the world by lust. ⁵ Now for this very reason also, **applying all diligence**, *in your faith supply moral excellence, and in your moral excellence, knowledge, ⁶ and in your knowledge, self-control, and in your self-control, perseverance, and in your perseverance, godliness, ⁷ and in your godliness, brotherly kindness, and in your brotherly kindness, love. ⁸ For if these qualities are yours and are increasing, they render you neither useless nor unfruitful in the true knowledge of our Lord Jesus Christ. ⁹* **For he who lacks these qualities is blind or short-sighted**, *having forgotten his purification from his former sins. ¹⁰ Therefore, brethren, be all the more diligent to make certain about His calling and choosing you; for as long as you* **practice these things, you will never stumble**; *¹¹ for in this way the entrance into the eternal kingdom of our Lord and Savior Jesus Christ will be abundantly supplied to you.* **2 Peter 1:1-11.**

We can say that our understanding, insight, discernment, learning, knowledge, and the application of all those things wisely must come through the filter of the Bible and the leading, prompting, guiding, and correcting of God the

Holy Spirit. This is so because it is through the Bible that we learn who God is and what He has said to us. It is the Holy Spirit who reveals God to us and who gives us understanding of the things of God, even insight into the Bible. 1 Corinthians 2:6, 10-13 gives us these truths:

> *Yet we do speak wisdom among those who are mature; a wisdom, however, not of this age nor of the rulers of this age, who are passing away. For to us God revealed them* **through the Spirit; for the Spirit searches all things, even the depths of God.** *For who among men knows the thoughts of a man except the spirit of the man which is in him? Even so the thoughts of God no one knows except the Spirit of God. Now we have received, not the spirit of the world, but the Spirit who is from God,* **so that we may know the things freely given to us by God,** *which things we also speak, not in words taught by human wisdom, but in those* **taught by the Spirit**, *combining spiritual thoughts with spiritual words.*

So, what we must keep in mind is that being a believer in the Lord Jesus Christ is much more than apprehending knowledge, even more than believing certain data. Believers are to put into action what they say they believe. James famously said that faith without works is useless and dead (James 2:20, 26), and we know that the enemy of our souls and his cohorts have the knowledge of the Father and the redemption He offers through faith in the Son and tremble (James 2:19).

This is why it is of utmost importance that believers "see" what it is they are to make actionable. A life lived for the glory of God is a life that is guided by the truth of God as revealed in the Bible and administered by the Holy Spirit.

The question thus becomes, who made your glasses? In other words, where did your understanding of the world and how it operates come from? What informed you of a proper response to the world system? Do you think and act subjectively or objectively? Is your view of the world as it exists today informed by your own ideas, attitudes, and understanding or is your view of the world and your responses to it shaped by something outside of yourself?

Do you submit yourself, bend your knee, and adhere to the precepts, statutes, commands, and principles that God has revealed to us through His revelation to us that is the Holy Scriptures? Do you apply with all diligence the things the Holy Spirit impresses upon you and shows you? Do you practice those things? Are these things consistent with what the Bible says?

If your beliefs lead you away from faith that grows deeper and more mature over time, if your doctrine does not help you develop a richer appreciation for Christ and what the Bible teaches then you must reconsider what you believe. You must submit yourself to the authority of the Bible, not make the Bible subservient to you. This is a huge issue today among people who profess faith in Jesus Christ.

Friends, it is not nearly enough to believe you have proper

doctrine and theology. People with opposing viewpoints, different glasses to carry the metaphor forward, believe they see things crystal clear. But this cannot be stated any clearer than I am about to now: if your theology, your doctrine, and living out the things you say you believe do not result in your own sanctification then something is amiss. If your doctrine and theology do not result in action then you are deceived. If your doctrine does not result in preaching the Gospel to the lost then what good is it?

Today we have Christians who believe that God approves of transgenderism, transsexuality, homosexuality, lesbianism, and now even pedophilia. Those same people, who believe they are showing God's love, march under the rainbow banner of sexual debauchery. Some people who believe their glasses provide 20/20 vision support the advocacy of the slaughter of unborn human beings. These same people support drag queens, Islamic indoctrination, homosexual normalization, and the destruction of our Western Civilization being advocated in the government schools. The very foundations of America are being systematically destroyed and many professing Christians are yielding the sledge hammers by blind ignorance and a Disneyland version of Christianity that renders them spiritually impotent to raise a single objection to the wholesale carnage being inflicted upon America.

It is time for true Christians as differentiated from Christians In Name Only (CINO's), to rise and push back hard against this darkness that has gripped America. If the way you see the world – your glasses – does not show you that America is dying at the hands of liberal progressive Marxists, neoconservatives, anarchists, atheists, wiccans, new agers, socialists, politicians of every party or no party, nihilists, narcissists, and apostate fake Christians operating in what has become the beast religious system of the last days one world religion, then it is time for you to get a new prescription! Throw those glasses away because your spiritual eyesight and therefore your soul is in peril. You are very close to becoming completely blind to what God is shouting at His people today.

Unless God makes your glasses you will ultimately become completely blind and worthless and will be tossed out and trampled underfoot by the stampede of God-haters that are on the march in America today. Will you take action? A visit to the eye doctor is as simple and easy as crying out to the One who gave you spiritual sight in the first place. May God have mercy on us and grant us the courage and determination to take our place in the widening breach the enemy of our souls has created in America.

Chapter Eight

"Who's God?"

During the Civil War Abraham Lincoln was asked whether he thought God was on the side of the North. After a few moments of thought the grim-faced Lincoln replied, "The real question is not whether God is on our side, but whether we are on God's side."

Churches today must face the same question. Are we calling on God to be on our side – whatever that may be – or are we joining God's side? Put another way, have we constructed gods of our own making to serve our needs or are we serving the God of the Bible? God asks, *"To whom then will you compare me, or who is my equal* (Isaiah 40:25).

Author Don McCollough suggests that many churches today have created either a "god-of-my-cause, a god-of-my-understanding, or a god-of-my-experience" that fills the void left by an abandonment of God and of true Christianity.

The "god-of-my-cause" manifests itself when churches begin with what they believe to be a good and worthy cause (liberation and feminist theologies come to mind immediately) and ends up using God to justify their participation. This re-casting of God into the mold of the cause is tantamount to fashioning a new calf of social righteousness.

The "god-of-my-understanding" is a vile and demonic representation of Christianity. Denominationalism is at its roots responsible for much of the strife and hostility seen in the church today. Doctrinal lines are drawn in the sand, enemies named and challenged, and theological self-assuredness abounds. Yet as McCollough points out, Christians forget that God is not contained in any theological system. Indeed, theological endeavors demand humility as much as critical thinking.

Finally, the "god-of-my-experience" has intercepted the movement of the Holy Spirit in many congregations. Churches are locked into *my* form of worship, *my* style of prayer, *my* focus in service. This mentality squeezes the life out of the body. The subjective rules over the objective, style wins over substance. The result is that Christians become "ingrown" and narrow-minded.

What can be done to overcome such tendencies? First, we must understand that a god we wish to fashion to fit our cause is ultimately no bigger than ourselves. Secondly, we must accept that this god cannot save us from our sins. Third, we must understand that any god that does not free us from the prison of our *individual* perspectives is nothing but a construct of our minds.

Chapter Nine

Has the Supreme Court Said?

Friends I have deliberately taken some time to consider the Supreme Court decision that created legislation making homosexual marriage legal in all fifty states. I want to address this in as clear a fashion as possible.

One thing that has become painfully apparent to me is that the Christian Church in America and by that I mean the big "C" Church, has been deceived into believing that life would continue on like it has always been and our Disneyland existence in the land of milk and honey would go on uninterrupted indefinitely.

On what do I base this assessment you ask? It is based in part on the exasperation and in some cases despair that abounds in American Christendom in response to the June 26, 2015 Supreme Court decision that effective created legislation out of thin air. Calling the Supreme Court decision vacuous and devoid of any legal standing is too kind. Chief Justice John Roberts, who of late has been a tremendous disappointment to those of us hoping for a return to sanity in political and cultural life in America, did get one thing right concerning the homosexual marriage debacle when he stated "The Constitution had nothing to do with it."

How have we arrived at a place that clearly represents a seismic shift in the moral foundation of a nation founded upon the Judeo-Christian faith and ethic? The place we find ourselves in as Americans is the result of a long and deliberate orchestration by the enemies of Christ. Their perseverance in undermining and effectively destroying the influence of Christianity has resulted in the rotten fruit we now see in America and which in my view has marked the beginning of the end for Christianity as a molder and shaper of culture. Voicing this perspective has resulted in me being labeled as a defeatist and unbiblical. The opposite is actually true. Let me explain.

A people or nation who tolerates evil will become numb to its presence and influence over time. What was once unthinkable becomes the norm. Once a new norm is achieved a new evil is advocated and it in turn soon becomes the new norm. This is a process of change employed by the enemies of Christ with much effectiveness. Hegel defined this process in his dialectic philosophy and it has been employed masterfully in

America. Proof of this is found in the number of Americans who rushed to the defense of Planned Parenthood when it was revealed that they are cannibalizing babies in the womb in order to harvest their organs for sale on the medical marketplace.

Romans chapter one speaks to this process. Please note that when a people become so deceived that they believe evil is enlightenment or to use the current subterfuged verbiage "tolerance and inclusiveness," God will turn them over to pursue this line of reasoning and behavior as well as all the detrimental results that arise from this thinking and behavior. No less than three times we are told that pursuing evil results in God allowing people to gorge themselves on it until they arrive at a place where they are unable to do anything else.

I see the members of the Supreme Court who voted in favor of creating homosexual marriage legislation as well as those who argued for its creation and even those tares among the wheat who celebrated this evil, being described in Romans 1:32 with these words: "and although they know the ordinance of God, that those who practice such things are worthy of death, they not only do the same, but also give hearty approval to those who practice them." The Supreme Court's decision to force the evil of homosexual marriage upon America is the moral equivalent of "giving hearty approval to those who practice" this sin.

It is time for the Remnant to rise up and be the Church God intends His people to be. It will require much change and most all of this change is going to come with a cost. When you challenge the evil power presiding over America you can expect nothing less than an evil response.

Gone are the days of assuming respectability within your communities because you're a Christian and you "just want to love people." This type of sentimentality masquerading as Christian faith will not stand the rigors of challenge by the ungodly. Perhaps that is why many professing Christians have made the serious error of capitulation and acceptance of this sin.

While you were sleeping Christian, the world changed the definition of love by removing any aspects of truth and righteousness. Those characteristics now belong in the realm of pure subjectivity and thus beyond the reach of any objective moral standard.

While Christians have been cloistered Sunday after Sunday learning how to be better husbands, wives, parents, coaches, friends to their neighbors, etcetera ad nauseum, the world has been fed a steady diet of anti-Christian hatred and now sees Christian beliefs and values as a liability to modern life and worthy of marginalization as much as possible. Look around the world today and you see the results – more oppressive laws restricting expressions of Christian faith, government intrusions upon the Church's rightful place of authority, rewriting the history of America to exclude the foundations of Christianity, and the ultimate expression of hatred - Christian martyrs.

What can Christians do in this brave new world being fashioned by the god-haters in America who now clearly have the law on their side? The answer may surprise you but I believe it is time to rejoice. Not rejoice in the escalating evil all around us but rejoice that God has counted you worthy to have eyes that see and ears that hear the Master calling you to active mission. Even in these new dark days God still desires to save people from their sin and He desires to use you in that work.

Secondly, resolve to stand firm in your faith and to contend earnestly for the faith even more so than before knowing that God is actively identifying those who have left the faith, those who have denied the faith, those who were really tares among the wheat. The Church has suffered for far too long because of ungodly leadership, fellowship, and misguided, misplaced ministry. Rejoice that God is marking these things so that the mission of Christ on this earth can be more effective and less impeded in this day.

Finally, never give up your hope. Instead always be ready to give a reason for why you hope in Christ. In the midst of the darkest hour the glory of God shines the brightest. Be ready to share the gospel of Jesus Christ with those who are bound up by sin. There will be many who will leave the homosexual lifestyle behind when they discover its empty promise of happiness and joy. Be ready to help put lives back together again with a message of forgiveness and mercy to all who will turn from their sin.

The serpent questioning God's Word set in motion a dramatic shift in the created order which resulted in judgment upon evil and a promise of a deliverer. Has the Supreme Court really said that homosexual marriage is normal and right? Challenging God's Word will bring judgment upon this evil and a reminder for the Remnant – stand firm for your redemption draws near.

Chapter Ten

Sowing and Reaping in Modern America

"You have plowed wickedness, you have reaped injustice. You have eaten the fruit of lies." Hosea 10:13a

America has been on a spiritual slide into darkness for many years. At first barely perceptible, the slide is now apparent to all but the most demonically oppressed and possessed who are blinded to the grievous condition we find ourselves in today. Unfortunately this blindness includes many who consider themselves Christians.

Although I could chronicle myriad examples from decades ago let me start with some of the most recent outrageous and wicked examples of this spiritual slide. Exhibit number one is the Kathy Griffin stunt concerning President Trump that was immediately condemned by most people. The recent apostasy of Hank Hanegraaff into Eastern Orthodoxy and compromise of James White with Islam provide more proof. Next consider the shooting of Congressman Scalise and other staffers in Washington DC. As a last example I offer you a video game that is set to be released soon called Far Cry 5. All of these seemingly disparate examples are tied together by the verse in Hosea cited above.

The context of this verse in Hosea is God's stated displeasure with Israel because of her continued rebellion. This rebellion is portrayed throughout the book within the theme of marriage and the patience of God through the long years of Israel's spiritual adultery. Among Israel's many sins were her practices of pagan idolatry, her trust in political alliances, and her social immorality where this continued open defiance of God was acceptable.

As pastor of a small church in fly-over country, I have watched with amazement the rapid transformation of America. Mr. Obama was a prophet in that he told Americans that he was going to fundamentally change America by offering us "change we can believe in." The devil certainly was in the details and only the spiritually awake Christian understood in his or her spirit that this change was not going to be good. For eight long years I watched Mr. Obama serve as a portal to elevate evil and to lead the charge to enshrine evil as public policy.

One of the many truths that Christians fail to grasp today is that the progress that Progressivism offers is not progress toward stability, peace, or national wellbeing, but progress away from God. Progressivism is an intellectual cancer that destroys any understanding of God-centered morality and His objective truth that alone can guide a nation through the turmoil of ungodly national inclinations produced when God-haters and pawns of Satan gain influence. America has become like Israel in that we have plowed wickedness and we are most certainly reaping the consequences.

The examples I cited above are all related in that they are symptoms of wickedness. Griffin has been spewing hatred for years toward Christians and disdain for a God she doesn't believe exists. At every step of the way her behavior has been applauded by certain segments of our society and resulted in her elevated status simply because of her evil bantering. In other words Griffin gained fame because of her hatred for God and Christians. In an effort to maintain her house of cards existence Griffin had to rely on a steady offering of increased evil that culminated recently in what should be a career destroying move.

Hanegraaff's apostasy was not unexpected as he has shown signs of unorthodoxy for some time. Eastern Orthodoxy is not orthodox Christianity but you would never know that from the multitudes that came to Hanegraaff's defense. Such muddled thinking is one reason why much of the visible Church has fallen into apostasy.

White's recent acquiescence to a radical Islam represented by Imam Yasir Qadhi is perhaps the most surprising of all. But on the other hand no one is beyond falling into error. That's why the Scriptures repeatedly warn us against following fallible man. White's delusion has been entertained by many before him such as Rick Warren. Believing that dialogue with God-hating, Jesus denying, psychotic women abusers will pave the way for these murderous Jihadi beasts to accept Christ as Savior is beyond alarming. It is outright naivety at a point in time when the strength of the gospel is most needed.

The attempted murder of Scalise in broad daylight is perhaps the most stunning illustration of the political hatred that has been fomented by Progressives, race-baiters, and social justice miscreants for years. As appalling as this attempted murder is, Progressives such as CBS News' Scott Pelley had the temerity to suggest that Scalise brought this on himself. In Pelley's mind people who have a different perspective on moral issues than Progressives should not be surprised when more enlightened people want to murder them. As many have observed previously, the Progressivism that has captured the Democratic Party and its stepchildren Antifata, Black Lives Matter, Media Matters, as well as many more organizations, is a brain destroying anti-philosophy of moral depravity and evil without basis in reality.

One final example for your consideration involves a video game. The creators of Far Cry 5 are set to roll out a new version of their video game which will focus on the hunting down and murder of Christians. Of course the Christians being hunted are the radical, fringe, cultic Christians; the kind that everyone should despise and hate to the degree that their extermination becomes a civic duty. Germans were fed this same propaganda in the 1930's and it resulted in deaf mutes that looked the other way while untold numbers of people were murdered.

Folks, here is the bottom line. America has become a captured operation. Our government is not by the people and it certainly is not for the people. Any viewpoint that is out of step with the new Progressive government handlers is being systematically outlawed. Hate speech laws give a legal foundation for future prosecution. All that remains is a perfect test case to spring it into action. A new Christianity is being shaped that is non-confrontational and culturally accepting and acceptable. This is a Christ-less form of pseudo-Christianity that is really not Christianity at all. Americans are being deceived into believing that viewpoints based on personal responsibility, an objective moral standard of right and wrong, and the belief that behaviors contrary to the Bible are sin, should be systematically persecuted and prosecuted. Christianity is quickly becoming anathema.

This explains the recent vitriolic rant by Senator Bernie Sanders against Russell Vought's confirmation as deputy director of the White House Office of Management and Budget? What makes Vought such a distasteful candidate in Sanders' mind? Vought is guilty of being a devout Christian and in Sanders' universe that is a high crime which renders Vought and anyone else with similar beliefs unworthy of any government position.

The stage is set for a clash between right and wrong. The culture wars are reaching a fevered pitch. Demonstrations have a taken a decidedly violent turn. Progressives have unrelentingly attacked free speech such that today on most college campuses students are the first to march for censorship. How times have changed since the 1960's when students marched for free speech.

As a pastor and watchman, it is my responsibility to say that the enemy is within the gates. The chaff is being separated from the wheat. The remnant is being identified. Take heart Christian and stand firm in your faith against this encroaching darkness. Put on the full armor of God and use the authority you have in Jesus Christ to rebuke the evil and warn the wicked to repent.

Chapter Eleven

"Missionaries to America"

My message to you via this article is a call to action. Let me give you a frame of reference with a large dash of levity.

"Come listen to my story 'bout a man named Jed.

A poor mountaineer, barely kept his family fed.

Then one day, he was shootin' at some food,

And up through the ground came a bubbling crude.

Black Gold, Texas Tea.

Well, the first thing you know ol' Jed's a millionaire.

Kin folk said Jed, move away from there.

Said, Californy is the place you ought to be,

So he loaded up the truck and moved to Beverly,

Hills that is. Swimmin' pools, movie stars.

Anyone remember that theme song? What was the show? Hard to believe that the Beverly Hillbillies was THE top rated television program for 2 of its 9 years on the air; it spend several years as a top 5 rated program, and it was ranked in the top 10 every year. That's mega-success by television standards.

- Did you know the Beverly Hillbillies received 7 Emmy Award nominations?
- Did you know that the Beverly Hillbillies had two spin-offs – Petticoat Junction and Green Acres?
- Here's another piece of trivia – Americans loved the show but television reviewers - the "critics" - hated it.

It's not hard to understand why the critics hated the show. The Beverly Hillbillies presented an America and Americans that had a conscience that subscribed to a Judeo-Christian morality and perspective on life, even though the script writers rarely mentioned God, Jesus, or the Bible. And the two spin-offs – Petticoat Junction and Green Acres followed the same script of wholesome values and moral teachings.

But in the 1960s Hollywood was changing. It wasn't obvious to most Americans then, but the "enlightened" critics wanted television to be a vehicle for social revolution. Hollywood even in those days was becoming a hub for anti-American values and they especially hated

Christianity.

Let me take you back to that era for a moment. The Beverly Hillbillies aired from 1962 – 1971. Those were the days weren't they? In 1962 I was in the 1ˢᵗ grade so it was a long time ago. Let's take a quick stroll down memory lane.

In 1962 America's children were still:

- Praying to God each day in the government school system.
- Reading their Bible each day in the government school system.
- Still being taught biblical creationism in the government school system.

Pastors were warmly greeted and asked to pray at sporting events, high school graduation ceremonies, civic organizations, school board meetings, city council meetings, and many other events.

When the Beverly Hillbillies aired the wholesale slaughter of unborn children upon the demonic altar named "choice" was unconscionable.

When Jed, Granny, Ellie Mae, and Jethro Bodine entertained Americans with their homespun wisdom and thinly-veiled Christian morality, we didn't have naked men, women, and children, dressed in the most sadomasochistic attire parading in our streets and celebrating their "pride." Brothers and sisters hear me clearly – there is nothing to be proud about what men do sexually to other men or what women do sexually to other women.

America of the 1960's my brothers and sisters, has been deliberately destroyed and a new America has risen from its ashes. We have gone from:

- Leave It To Beaver to the number one on demand video platform – Netflix – offering pornography available to anyone including children.
- We have gone from Happy Days where the trouble teenagers got into was drag racing in the streets, to Antifa which is bringing bloodshed to our streets.

Would you agree that America 2018 is a broken and crippled nation, far removed from the vision of our Founding Fathers?

Now, the question that I must ask at this point is this – What are we going to do? What are we going to do to change the trajectory of America? What are we going to do to push back against the darkness that has a stranglehold on the throat of America and is systematically choking the life out of this nation?

Here's what we cannot do friends – we cannot continue to skip down the yellow brick road to Oz, thinking that it will all work itself out in the end.

We cannot trust that our eschatology will save us. Can I give you a word of encouragement here friends? Stop fussing about the rapture! Here's another word for you — stop arguing about what day we are required to honor God on.

You are not more spiritual or closer to God based on what day you set aside to honor Him. You are not more biblically rooted and prophetically astute based on your view of the rapture timing.

And speaking of our holy huddles — whatever day you choose to honor God on — we have to stop thinking that gathering together with our brothers and sisters one day a week constitutes our service for God.

What about the other 6.5 days? What about James' admonition that faith without works is dead? What about the Apostle Paul's admonition to be living sacrifices to Christ daily, and to demonstrate that by being transformed in our thinking? Are we only to have transformed minds one day a week?

If you have your Bible with you today, turn with me to Acts 1:1-8. This is a familiar passage to most everyone. Different people focus on different things when they read the Bible. Here's what I want you to see from this passage.

Take note that in V4-5 God gives us power. The same power that raised Jesus from the dead lives in us. Some people ignore this power because they are more concerned about a proper theology and especially a proper view of the end times. That's exactly the mindset of the disciples as stated in V6.

Remember my word of encouragement a few moments ago to stop arguing about eschatology? Jesus says the same thing in V7. Don't worry about it. The Father has it under control.

Here's what we need to be concerned about according to Jesus – V8.

What do we see in this passage? I see at least three things for you to remember. They are:

(1) Receive the Holy Spirit's power.

- This is the power necessary to conquer the onslaught of evil in our day.
- This is the power that gives us boldness and unflinching courage.

(2) We are told that we must be Christ's witnesses.

- Do you understand that this means we are to represent Him as He is not how the culture demands He be? Jesus is not a rainbow flag waving, socialist!
- Do you understand that this means we are to proclaim everywhere that only Jesus saves and that we are to do this without apology or compromise?

(3) We are to tell our family, friends, co-workers, and fellow citizens of the town that we live in first. We must start in our Jerusalem and only when our Jerusalem is saturated are we to move beyond that place.

- There is more than enough work to be done to repair the breaches in the communities that we live in. We don't need to look for opportunities elsewhere.
- Expect push back from your family, friends, co-workers, and fellow Christians. Keep making your case anyway.

Now, I want you to consider this passage in Acts 1 with the picture I've already painted courtesy of the Beverly Hillbillies.

The Beverly Hillbillies were television missionaries to America and they were rejected. The show was cancelled while it was a top rated show. It was cancelled because America as it existed then was detested and hated primarily for its Christian roots. The message of the show was no longer acceptable to those who had the power to silence it.

So, this melting pot that was once America, was refashioned for another purpose – that purpose was to slowly boil frogs. Let me say that again - The melting pot that was America was re-purposed for a single purpose and that was to boil frogs. Guess who the frogs are friends? That's right, the frogs being boiled are true Christians.

Let me tell you what has happened while Christians have enjoyed their sauna hot tub pot:

- Homosexuals and Lesbians are now marrying AND a large portion of the so-called Christian church celebrates that with them. Let me say this as clearly and as frankly and as pointedly as I can – if you belong to a gay-affirming church then get out of that place immediately, for you are residing in Sodom.
- Coach Dave Daubenmire, David Arthur, and others went to a Gay Pride parade not long ago in Columbus, Ohio. You want to know who argued with them the most about being accepting of the sin of sexual depravity? Other professing Christians!

While the frogs swim around in their heated pool:

- Human sex trafficking has become an epidemic.

While the frogs sip their iced tea and talk about their favorite pastimes:

- Pedophilia is being mainstreamed. That is to say the Luciferians among us are doing everything they can to normalize this abomination.
- Satanic ritual abuse is out in the open. Worshipping Satan is trendy.

We can look to Washington DC to do something but friends, politicians are not going to save us. We already have a Savior and it's high time we remember that fact and then act upon the power we already have.

I may offend some people here (or maybe it's too late) but I wonder why churches spend millions of dollars every year for foreign missions when America is a stinking, rotting shell of what it once was?

Our cities are war zones; heroin deaths are at an all-time high; alcohol has become the anesthetic of choice and Washington DC pounds a constant drum beat that law abiding citizens are the problem so let's take their guns, let's take their freedom of speech and let's take their freedom of assembly and worship and America will be great again!

Friends we are being played!! While Christians gather weekly for a time of clapping and shouting and congratulating ourselves for the wonderful lives we have allegedly because of God's favor, our Federal Government continues to undermine the safety and prosperity of our nation through their incessant immigration policies. The globalists who control our government dispatch our armed forces all over the world to guard oil and opium fields from those nasty terrorists, to destabilize the governments of countries that refuse to play by our rules, and then allow hundreds of thousands of those same people into our nation because it is the humanitarian thing to do!

Excuse me for playing Captain Obvious here – As Americans our primary mission field is not Haiti, Iraq, Afghanistan, or any other nation around the world. Our primary mission field is America. America is our Jerusalem. And if we ignore that, soon there will be no foundation left in America to reach out to foreign countries.

It is long past time for the true body of Christ to rise up and with holy vigor fight back against the onslaught of evil in our time. Here is what I suggest you take to heart and then start action planning about how you are going to get in the fight.

(1) Understand that being saved is the beginning not the end.

Christians must move beyond throwing money at ministries who do the things they are unwilling to do, to actually doing ministry in the streets.

- Join with other believers who are going to abortion clinics, prisons, county jails, half-way houses, and drug infested neighborhoods. Ask your pastor to start leading the flock to do these things.
- Christian parent – if you want your son or daughter to experience a different culture while ministering to the poverty stricken and oppressed just pick a city – any city in America, and you'll find a new cultural experience ministering to people who desperately need it.

(2) Get equipped with the WORD OF GOD.

This is more of a challenge than it used to be. A recent Barna Group survey of professing Christians who consider themselves regular church attendees were asked this question: "Do you know what the Great Commission is?" Here are the responses:

- 51% said no, never heard of it.
- 25% said yes, I've heard of it but I don't know what it is.
- 17% said yes I know what it is.
- 6% were not sure.

Let me do the math for you – 76% of professing believers didn't know or couldn't explain what the Great Commission is.

Jesus said "If you continue in My word, then you are truly disciples of mine; and you will know the truth and the truth will make you free." (John 8:31-32)

Here's the problem we are facing today friends: People have abandoned the Word of God but they still want to appear spiritual, so they become fake Christians.

AW Tozer wrote:

> The difficulty we modern Christians face is not misunderstanding the Bible, but persuading our untamed hearts to accept its plain instructions.

The late Pastor Chuck Smith said:

> There is a real battle for the Bible taking place in our world today. The battle isn't necessarily outside the church, between those who don't believe in God and

those in the church who do believe in God. Sadly, the battle for the Bible is found within the church, even with some pastors leading the attack against the Bible.

Christians simply must get back to a robust study of the Bible and obedience to what it says. It is timeless, speaking to every heart of every person if given the chance. It is never out dated or irrelevant. IF you are in a church in which the pastor rarely teaches from the Bible or sugar-coats most everything, or refuses to speak to the issues facing America today then please run! Get out of that place and find a faithful body of believers.

That the enemies of God spend so much time and energy attacking the Bible should serve as all the motivation a believer needs to cling tightly to it. If the enemies of God hate the Bible then you must know it is invaluable to believers today.

(3) Organize with other like-minded believers.

Distance used to be an obstacle but not anymore. Start getting involved with other believers and their activism.

Coach Dave Daubenmire has a good model that is working and I suggest you speak with him about how to set up a network in your area. You can email him ptsalt@gmail.com

You may have to start a Bible study yourself, if you can't find a local church that is faithful to the Father and His Word.

(4) Become an activist. We must tell our elected representatives that God will hold them accountable for their actions or inactions, whatever the case may be.

Listen friends, we are not going to be a majority in America. But we don't need a majority. We need a vocal, irate minority.

God established government to be a servant of the people, to prevent evil, and to promote righteousness. It is our duty to remind people of that truth.

That might require you to visit your mayor, city council, county commissioner, school board or sheriff.

You might need to go to your state capital and seek a meeting with your state representative, and even the governor of the state in which you live.

One thing we must not do is remain silent because we believe there is nothing we can do to change anything. That's not the point friends.

Giving our testimony to those who claim to be public servants of the righteous and holy King who will judge this wicked generation, is the point.

Remember these words: Romans 8:37 – We are more than conquerors through Him who loved us.

That means:

- We are never alone – Jesus said, I will not leave you as orphans. I will come to you.
- We have already overcome through Christ – so be courageous in doing your duty because Jesus has already overcome the world.
- We have a blessed hope – this world system is going to crash and burn when Jesus returns. But until He does our job is to occupy and fight the good fight with the full armor God has given to us.

The Beverly Hillbillies were missionaries to a people that believed their (1) wealth (2) position (3) power made God irrelevant. Hollywood rejected that message then and America is rejecting it today.

The Hillbillies were fish out of water but they persisted. And week after week Mr. Drysdale and Ms. Hathaway learned valuable life lessons that pointed them to the foundation of all truth – the Lord Jesus Christ.

That America was murdered right in front of our eyes. Do we have the courage to challenge this ongoing demonic war for the souls of American men and women?

I pray that we do. We are watchmen. Watchmen warn. It's too late to warn of impending danger. The enemy is already within the gates, and is wreaking havoc in every aspect of our shared cultural lives.

But we must still warn people to repent and turn to God.

Brothers and sisters, if you take away nothing else from what I have said please understand this – God will require an accounting of how we used the talents He gives to His people. May we be found faithful in service to King Jesus.

Let us go to our families, friends, neighbors, coworkers, churches, and communities with a freshly kindled fire and Holy Spirit energized passion to serve King Jesus in things that matter eternally.

Chapter Twelve

Flipping Congress by the Power of Beelzebul

But when the Pharisees heard this, they said, "This man casts out demons only by Beelzebul the ruler of the demons." Matthew 12:24

If I by Beelzebul cast out demons, by whom do your sons cast them out? For this reason they will be your judges. Jesus Christ in Matthew 12:27

A recent article posted at The Huffington Post by religion reporter Carol Kuruvilla announced the group Vote Common Good (VCG), was beginning a bus tour to selected cities in America to challenge conservative evangelical Christian support for President Trump.

Who and what is Vote Common Good and what issues do they see as problematic for Christians supporting President Trump specifically and the Republican Party generally? Not surprisingly the "who" of Vote Common Good reads like a progressive, leftist, Marxist list of who's who. The Executive Director of VCG is Doug Pagitt, he of the once dubbed Emerging Church movement, and author of *An Emergent Manifesto of Hope*, among other books.

Kuruvilla quotes Pagitt giving readers his motivation for steering VCG: "Evangelicals care about the least of these, and I believe them when they say it...but they vote for politicians that invoke policies that don't care for the least of these." Here Pagitt is being deceitful either through his personal ignorance or deliberate obfuscation concerning the issue of immigration. Either way this is social gospel 101 which is to say not the biblical gospel.

The social gospel takes biblical language such as "the least of these" and super charges it with progressive Marxist meaning and liberation theology. Kuruvilla admits as much when she says that Pagitt and other Progressive Christians "are outraged by the Trump administration's restrictive refugee policies and its separation of immigrant families at the U.S.-Mexico border..." For Progressive Christians like Pagitt, their silence during eight long years of the reign of the Obama regime, who enforced the very same rules and laws concerning immigration, is a condemning indictment against their faux rage with President Trump and Republicans, and this makes the foundation for VCG disingenuous in the least.

Pagitt and his cohorts' carefully choreographed meltdown over the current media driven crisis concerning immigration is better suited for Broadway than it is for national discussion. Nevertheless, true Christians should take this opportunity to give solid biblical reasons for why we must oppose what the left, masquerading as Christians is attempting to do. The reason I say this is: (1) Immigration MUST be regulated. A nation simply cannot and should not allow for mass invasion by whoever shows up at its borders. (2) There must be a vetting process for the safety of a nation's citizens which its government is bound by law and morals to protect as a primary mission. (3) God has established sovereign nations, and recognizable borders and the enforcement of them is consistent with God's design.

Sometimes open borders advocates such as Pagitt, McLaren, Wallis, and Clairborne, quote scriptural passages such as Exodus 23 or Deuteronomy 10 that admonish God's people to be kind to the foreigner who was living amongst them (Exod. 23:9; Lev. 19:34; Deut. 10:19). These exhortations are merely referring to basic compassion toward the less fortunate in their midst. These less fortunate were those who were foreigners and yet legal citizens of the nation of Israel. They were not immigrants. Context is everything in biblical interpretation but Pagitt and VCG don't want people to know that because their position is much more palatable to people who do not know the truth of what the Bible actually says.

Bryan Fischer, a commentator on American Family Radio has said, "No one has a constitutional or moral right to immigrate to the United States. The Constitution gives

Congress unilateral authority to decide under what conditions those from foreign lands are admitted into our country."

Something else is clearly at work here.

That something else is the destruction of orthodox Christianity. Pagitt along with co-conspirators Brian McLaren, John Pavlovitz, Reverend Jacqui Lewis, Shane Claiborne, and Nadia Bolz-Weber, whom Kuruvilla names as "prominent progressive Christian pastors...authors, ministers and activists," involved in promoting the VCG tour left orthodox Christianity a long time ago. They are now on a mission to destroy true Christianity from the inside out. They are in fact the tares the enemy planted in the wheat field of God's people. "Progressive" Christian is an oxymoron. We could just as easily call them "Fascist" Christian or "Marxist" Christian.

Their support for the Democrat Party is proof enough of that. Let me give some specifics of what Pagitt is encouraging Christians to support by his support of the Democrat Party:

- The redefinition of women's reproductive healthcare to mean the wholesale murder of unborn human beings up to the day of delivery from the mother's womb. Murdering babies is not healthcare it is momicide.
- This right to murder unborn human beings must include the most heinous practice of partial birth

abortion where the baby's head is positioned outside of the mother's vagina so that the baby's brains can be removed.

- The legal and moral sanction of men with men and women with women and the prosecution of anyone who dares voice disapproval.
- The normalization of pedophilia.
- Drag Queens, transgenderism, transsexualism, and every other sexual depravity being normalized to our children through government indoctrination centers commonly called public schools.
- Open borders for everyone showing up wanting access to America.
- Confiscation of all fire arms from law abiding citizens.
- Censorship of all viewpoints that oppose their party line.
- Advancing the demonic LBGT debauchery through foreign policy.
- Incorporation of Wicca, New Age, and Satan worshippers into the Democrat Party.
- Rejection of God and prayer from the national life of Americans and certainly the Democrat Party Platform.
- Forcing Americans to pay for everything the out of control US Federal Government can dream of.
- Advocating violence against fellow citizens because they hold a conservative viewpoint. See Waters, Clinton, Holder, et al.

- Government corruption during the Obama years including the unprovoked destruction of Libya, Egypt, and Syria.
- Doing away with the Electoral College that the founding fathers were wise enough to install to protect Americans against the tyranny they envisioned happening in present day California and New York.
- The purposeful and with malice, attempted destruction of people for no other reason than they hold to a different perspective on moral issues. Two words here: Judge Kavanaugh.

I could go on but the point is that what Pagitt and Vote Common Good is doing is telling people to vote Democrat and by extension to support the demonic behavior listed above and much more. Given the things that the Democrat Party stands for, it is beyond insanity to suggest Americans should support them, especially that Christians should support them. The talking points Pagitt and his supporters utilize are the same tired, meaningless, amorphous topics: the environment, poverty, healthcare, etc. etc. How can Pagitt and his supporters be so blind?

They are blind because what is at work here is supernatural. America is in the throes of a spiritual war manifesting in space and time. The Kavanaugh hearing was just the latest example of Luciferianism from the Democrats and their puppet masters. Pagitt and VCG are nothing more than zombie foot soldiers of the left in this war. Mike Adams has very succinctly stated:

> Realize this is not a political war but a spiritual war. The demon-possessed Leftists don't merely want to achieve political victory and rule society with "progressive" ideas; they seek to destroy humanity, obliterate human life, mass murder babies, outlaw Christianity, demonize people based on the color of their skin, and even decimate all crops, forests and food sources on the planet by eliminating CO_2 from the atmosphere. **They are at war with humanity,** and they merely pretend to be interested in politics as a means to accomplish their complete destruction of life on Earth.[2]

There is a reason why black Americans are leaving the Democrat Party by the thousands. There is a reason why the #walkaway movement is growing day by day. There is a reason why older Americans are leaving the party they have been a part of for decades. That reason is because the Democrat Party has become the party of Beelzebul. For those not familiar with the word, Beelzebul is Satan in the New Testament.

---

[2] Mike Adams, The REAL WAR for the future of humanity: Democrats increasingly possessed by demonic forces that seek the extermination of humanity? Accessed October 12, 2018 here - https://www.naturalnews.com/2018-10-10-democrats-possessed-by-demonic-forces-thought-experiment.html

The current and recent leadership of the Democrat Party has taken it not just to the left, not even a hard left, but an off the charts course change that has embraced every form of debauchery, every form of anti-American policy, every anti-Christian position imaginable. The Democrat Party is one manifestation of the spirit of antichrist in our day. Apparently Pagitt and other VCG adherents are on board with these things.

Pagitt is quoted in the article as saying: "My faith does not call me to be Republican or Democrat, but to be faithful, and to be faithful is exercise my right to action, according to the situation on the ground, and what's on the ground is calling us to flip Congress, because it is no good." Once again, this is nothing but lip service and propaganda aimed at disarming the naïve Christians among us. Pagitt is providing a religious cover for all those that wish to continue the activities of the Democrat Party listed above.

What Pagitt and VCG want is leftist, progressive, fascist governments that in their warped sense of reality will much better care for citizens, the less fortunate among us, and the environment. Maybe Pagitt could spend about two minutes in Venezuela and let us know what he thinks of leftist progressive government then.

The truth is Pagitt is not being faithful to biblical mandates either in precept or command. He is being faithful to his brainwashed version of reality where he thinks the goal of Christianity is to reshape the world into a paradise and he is ok attempting to use government to do it.

Pagitt needs to be reminded that this world is fallen. Sin has destroyed the original beauty this world was created in. Not until Christ returns will all things be set straight and made new. Only when Christ returns will evil be completely dealt with.

Yes, Christians should be assisting the less fortunate but not in isolation from the gospel. What Vote Common Good does is a disservice to the gospel and to Christianity. It is nothing but a political ploy which Pagitt and others claim they detest.

Claiming to be wise Pagitt shows himself to be a fool. The Democrat Party is unashamedly Luciferian in its intentions and in their stated goals. Its primary goal is to destroy Christianity and any lingering impact it has on America. In siding with them Pagitt and those who assist and support Vote Common Good are doing the work of Beelzebul whether they want to admit it or not.

Postscript

Those of you who are tempted to write me "yea, but the Republicans…" can save your breath. I don't support them either and the point of this article is to address Vote Common Good and the idiocy of following these blind guides of the blind. Christians should be rebuking VCG and its supporters starting with its leadership.

Chapter Thirteen

The Spirit of Antichrist, Christian Self-Flagellation, and Getting It Wrong

The Old Testament of the Bible contains many narratives that give instruction to the modern Christian. One such example is the story of the prophet Elijah and the evil King Ahab and Queen Jezebel.

In 1 Kings 21 we find the account of the King and Queen of Israel plotting to dispossess a man of his property. Deceit, lying, and libel were all employed expertly by Jezebel to cause the murder of the man Naboth. His crime? His desire to retain his land and vineyard and not sell them to the King. Naboth rightly stated that he was forbidden to sell his land to anyone because God had given it as an inheritance (21:3). Thus in seeking to obey and honor God Naboth became an enemy of the King and Queen.

Of particular interest in this story is the decree of God through the prophet Elijah to Ahab and Jezebel concerning their guilt and the judgment awaiting them as a result. Note verses 19-24 for the specific content of the judgment. Verse 22 is instructive for our purposes as it declares:

> "and I will make your house like the house of Jeroboam the son of Nebat, and like the house of Baasha the son of Ahijah, *because of the provocation with which you have provoked Me to anger, and because you have made Israel sin*" (italics added).

How did Ahab and Jezebel provoke God to anger? By sponsoring the worship of the demon known as Baal (1 Kings 16:30-33). Clearly the sin of idolatry was state sponsored. Elsewhere God held the people responsible for their idolatry but here in this passage He lays the blame squarely at the feet of Ahab and Jezebel.

What application can be made from this event for modern Christians? Several principals are suggested. First, the state should never support religious practices that dishonor God. Indeed the biblical prescription for government is that it concern itself almost solely with keeping the peace, providing safety to its citizens, rewarding good, and punishing evil. This last qualification of a government that God has established is very important. More on that later.

Second, the state cannot know the difference between good and evil apart from an understanding of God as expressed in the Christian theistic tradition. Contrary to the current postmodern mindset there is right and there is wrong and the standard for determining which is which resides outside of the individual.

Third, when the state rejects God it has nowhere else to turn but to idolatry and the establishment of laws and practices that lead its people to sin against God. State sponsorship of religious practices that are antithetical to Christian theism consequentially creates enemies of the state.

Fourth, God will not hold that state blameless which lead His people to sin. There will be a day of reckoning.

Finally but not least important, much can be accomplished if the righteous will stand against the wicked. We have the authority and power of Jesus Christ and it is high time we use it to push back against this evil and adulterous generation.

So why write this column? What inspired this idea of a connection between the spirit of Antichrist and the rampant Christian bent of self-flagellation and wrongfully attributing blame instead of rising up to oppose the present evil in our land? Quite simply friends, the number of people speaking condemnation upon the Church and articles being written by Christians that place the blame squarely upon the Church for the present evil that threatens to completely overtake America; that is what has given rise to this article.

Now let me state unequivocally that I understand that the American Church has much to repent of, not the least of which is the quest for power in conjunction with the state and the perverse attention given to a social gospel which is as the Apostle Paul stated another gospel. Our in-fighting over trivial matters is legendary. But the attitude of many in these dark days is that the mess we find ourselves in is solely on the Church for failing somehow to be the Church. I find this charge absurd and a great demonstration of just how blind people have become to the spirit of the age.

The increasing criticism that I hear from many different sources is that the Church is at fault when it comes to the social and cultural evils America is experiencing. Some Christians seem to be saying that this crisis could have been avoided if the Church would have been the Church. I'm not completely clear on what that catch phrase actually means – "if the Church would have been the Church" – but I believe these critics are attempting to say one of two things. Either that the Church has not done enough to stem the tide of evil and that if the Church would have done more in the past America would not be where it is today, or they could be saying that the Church really hasn't loved like Jesus loved and that is why there is so much evil. If this is what is meant then what we have is on one hand the Church has not demonstrated enough activism and on the other the Church has not shown enough compassion.

There is a Greek word that describes this misguided thinking – baloney! Are there examples of the Church failing to live out its beliefs? Many examples exist that critics point to in order to sustain the arguments above. But history shows that the Church has concerned itself with social issues, has responded with compassion to the needs of the helpless and the hopeless, and has been engaged culturally when no one else has. To suggest otherwise is to be willfully ignorant of the truth. Can we improve? There is much room for improvement to be sure but to throw out the entire history of the Church in America in one fell swoop is unconscionable.

But there is a greater point that must be discussed and one that is an impetus for this article. The Bible teaches that in the days before Christ's return the world which includes the Church will be a mess. For example:

> *"But the Spirit explicitly says that in later times some will fall away from the faith, paying attention to deceitful spirits and doctrines of demons, by means of the hypocrisy of liars seared in their own conscience as with a branding iron"*
> **(1 Timothy 4:1-2).**

"I solemnly charge you in the presence of God and of Christ Jesus, who is to judge the living and the dead, and by His appearing and His kingdom: preach the word; be ready in season and out of season; reprove, rebuke, exhort, with great patience and instruction. For the time will come when they will not endure sound doctrine; but wanting to have their ears tickled, they will accumulate for themselves teachers in accordance to their own desires, and will turn away their ears from the truth and will turn aside to myths" **(2 Timothy 4:1-4).**

"But realize this, that in the last days difficult times will come. For men will be lovers of self, lovers of money, boastful, arrogant, revilers, disobedient to parents, ungrateful, unholy, unloving, irreconcilable, malicious gossips, without self-control, brutal, haters of good, treacherous, reckless, conceited, lovers of pleasure rather than lovers of God, holding to a form of godliness, although they have denied its power; Avoid such men as these" **(2 Timothy 3:1-5).**

There is a common thread that runs through these passages. Note that the 1 Timothy 4 passage speaks of some within the Church losing faith because of the influence of spirits and demons and having rejected the Christian faith replace it with the hypocritical lies of spirits and demons. Please note here friends that you must not assume these people have left the Church. Verse 3 indicates they are still very much involved in the Church, so much so that they insist on celibacy among the brethren and strict dietary rules.

The 2 Timothy 4 passage shows what happens when false converts and apostates are allowed to remain in the body of Christ – they infect the entire body by rejecting the truth of God. Teachers and Preachers are charged by Paul to focus on preaching the Word of God in its entirety and to use the Word of God to reprove, rebuke, and exhort listeners. This passage clearly points out many will not listen and will seek out people who will tell them what they want to hear.

The 2 Timothy 3 passage also makes it clear that the Church will be challenged by worldly attitudes within. Godliness is a formality with no power. I believe this is a clear statement that many in the Church will be unregenerate, i.e. without the Holy Spirit (power).

So the challenge that the Church faces is not to be more like the culture (seeker sensitive). We are not to change our beliefs so that we can reach more people (emergent). We are not to adopt some kind of faux-compassion in order to be liked or accepted by the world (missional/social). These strategies are all the result of demonic invasion into the thinking of Christians and churches. But friends, if this thinking has invaded the Church then it is doing so from a position of strength, having already captured the culture in which we live.

The truth is that the spirit of Antichrist is palatable today. The recently deposed Obama monarchy manifested the clearest danger that the Church in America had ever faced. That statement is demonstrably true. At no time in our nation's history had any President or collection of so-called public servants demonstrated such a bitter hatred for the ideals, values, and teachings of Christianity. At no time had any President gone out of his way to establish depravity and ungodliness and to codify them as law. Mr. Obama was a god-hating leftist Marxist globalist and remains so to this day.

America's laws were established on the basis of Judeo-Christian beliefs. Our cultural mores and values all trace back to Christianity. The perversion and rejection of these beliefs has resulted in a broken legal system and cultural mayhem. Cherry-picking values and inserting personal opinions into legal proceedings have aided the evil we see today. The belief that pluralism is the antidote to what ails America is nonsense. But that is exactly the path both secularists and some misguided Christians are taking. Being open to COEXIST theology flies in the face of CONTRADICT truth (Some bumper sticker humor there).

I have to tell you friends that the numbers of believers who once held strong convictions and were not afraid to stand and speak truth is dwindling. I see articles from people I once respected that articulate the idea that the Church is the reason America is in dire straits. The cultural evil we are seeing in America is now somehow the fault of those of us who are speaking out about the political evil and march toward globalism that is running roughshod over individual liberty and freedom. This is some strong Orwellian gobbledygook going on here. Really it is some weird type of self-flagellation. Perhaps these folks think that if they guilt themselves or others enough the culture will take notice and like us or tell us that we are relevant once more. Acquiescing to the god-haters is a wrong-headed strategy and cannot be supported scripturally.

How is it the fault of the Church that the spirit of Antichrist has risen in the land? Does not the Bible say that this will happen in the time before the return of Christ? If it does, then why are so many Christians pointing their fingers at the Church? Isn't this a huge distraction and an unnecessary waste of time? Should the remnant take Paul's advice to Timothy and "avoid such men as these"?

Let me summarize a few points in conclusion.

(1) We must understand that this present government is not of God. Mr. Trump may well be sent by God as many have suggested. But the belly of the beast remains anti-Christian to the core. Do not hide behind the veneer of this lame statement: "Well God establishes governments so I must obey this government." Please read my previous posts on the topic of governments that God establishes here and here. The spirit of Antichrist is on

display. When Christians act as apologists for our government and its minions they divert attention from this evil in America and are doing a huge disservice to the Kingdom of God.

(2) Christians who think they can win the lost to Christ by being their friend are following a failed strategy. Where in the Bible are we called to befriend people in order to win them to Christ? I'm not saying that you can't be friends with the lost but the idea that evangelism incorporates that as a biblical norm is in error. Programs are not needed. The Gospel is needed.

(3) If Christians really want to impact the culture around us then we will quit supporting multi-million dollar ministries who fervently crow about the need for private jets, multi-million dollar mansions, and extravagant lifestyles all for Jesus' glory. If you really want to show the love of Christ then sell all you have, give to the poor, and follow Jesus.

(4) Judgment has come upon America. The rise of homosexuality, lesbianism, transgenderism, Satanism, and the continued worship of Moloch through the sacrificing of unborn children has helped created the mess America is neck-deep in today. But these are all just symptoms of the larger problem – the rise of the spirit of antichrist and the captivation of American society.

(5) The remnant of Christians today must band together.

Our brethren are being murdered all over the world. The American government is financing this genocide. If you think for a second that the same atrocities you see elsewhere will not touch America you are blind, naive, and might I say stupid. It is a special kind of ignorance that thinks Christians in America will not be touched by this evil.

(6) The real Church is still the Church and Christ said the gates of Hell will not prevail against it. The falling away of many into apostasy was prophesied. Those who have fallen away are not the Church so let's move on from constantly criticizing "the Church" when we are really talking about the apostates. The remnant does nothing but give the god-haters among us a perfect narrative to continue their ungodly assault upon us when we are given to constant criticism.

Friends please take the message of this post seriously. Time is growing short and there is still a lot of work to be done. If you've left the Church and meet in your home now then I encourage you to start inviting your neighbors to hear you teach the Bible. If you are in a church that does not teach the Bible then why are you still there? Friends, family, comfort? Get out of that place and find a church that teaches the Bible. Here's a piece of information for you when you begin to hunt for a new church – it won't be like what you left. If you find a church that is faithful to the Scriptures cling to it like glue because they are few.

Finally, evaluate your life. Where you've been, where you want to go in life, and why. Does your plan line up with Kingdom principles for the day we live in? Are you still pursuing the great American dream of bigger, better, and more? If so why? Being a servant of the King means doing things His way. Make sure you are.

My prayer for you is that you will rise above the blatant present evil and courageously put on God's armor every day and be a shining light for the Gospel of Jesus Christ today.

If you would like to know more about trusting Jesus Christ for the forgiveness of your sins and the receiving of a new and eternal life in Christ email me at:
drmichaelspaulding@gmail.com

Chapter Fourteen

Lead Like Jesus?

Lead like Jesus! Sounds super spiritual and to use today's hipster pastor language, "way cool!" There are blog posts, multiple articles, even books all dedicated to assisting readers in leading like Jesus lead. The question is what does that even mean?

In many instances today, authors, speakers, and writers paint a picture of the compassion, mercy, forgiveness, patience, tolerance, and unbounded grace of Jesus. While Jesus is all those things, it doesn't follow that is His leadership style. The fact is modern Western Christianity has created a sad caricature of the biblical Jesus.

In Mark 10:32 we read that Jesus and the disciples were on the road once again, this time to head to Jerusalem. This verse says "and Jesus was walking ahead of them, and they were amazed, and those who followed were fearful." The context of this passage and the place it sits within the overall narrative of Mark's Gospel is important to understand.

Jesus was now within a few weeks, perhaps as few as 4 to 6, from His divine appointment at Golgotha. Chapter 11:1 tells us Jesus and the disciples approached Jerusalem. Their entry into Jerusalem in verse 11 is what we call Palm Sunday. So the events we are reading about in Mark 10 are relevant to their arrival in Jerusalem and the rapid escalation of hatred that culminated in Calvary.

So, Jesus was walking ahead of the twelve disciples and they were amazed. Do you know why they were amazed? The text doesn't tell us specifically but I believe the twelve were amazed at the bold determination of Jesus to march right into the jaws of the beast that awaited Him in Jerusalem. The religious system of Judaism in that day was an apostate beast system of corruption, manipulation, and deceit. The Jews had been plotting to murder Jesus for at least the previous 18-24 months. They seethed with rage just thinking of His popularity among the people, and they had become convinced that unless Jesus was killed their entire religious business was going to collapse like an unstable house of cards.

In the events recorded in Mark 10, the Pharisees thought they had conceived of the perfect plan and that they had been patient enough to spring their trap when Jesus crossed over the Jordan into Perea ("beyond the Jordan" in 10:1). They deliberately brought up the issue of divorce thinking they could manipulate Jesus into getting Himself arrested based on His own words. The Pharisee's plan was to engage Jesus in a debate about divorce while He was traveling through the territory ruled by Herod Antipas. It was Herod Antipas who had John the Baptists' head removed. Do you recall why Herod took such action? John was jailed and executed because he spoke loud and often that Herod was an adulterer for stealing his brother's wife. But Jesus once again took them to theological school by teaching them God's thoughts on the subject.

Now, I'm stating all of this to show you the true nature of Jesus' leadership style. Friends, Jesus is not the effeminate Fabio caricature much of the American church thinks He is. Do you want to lead like Jesus? Then here is what you are going to need to do.

(1) You are going to have to lead the way. You are going to have to take the point. I know it has become popular to say that pastoral leadership is all about teaching others to do the ministry. The reality is others will follow and learn as you lead and do. But you better be very careful about how and where you lead God's people, especially if you are considered a shepherd. God will hold you personally responsible for the spiritual nourishment or lack thereof that His people receive.

(2) You are going to have to find some courage. Leading is not about having all the answers. Only Jesus had all the answers. Leading is about having a determination to meet evil head-on. This includes being courageous in the pulpit. Pastors and ministry leaders simply must stop all the cotton candy sermons about how much God loves people. The most glaring problem in the church today is not a lack of self-love. People already love themselves too much.

(3) You are going to have to stop listening to false teachers. Today we have well-known teachers, former and current pastors, and heads of denominational organizations who have succumbed to critical race theory propaganda, cultural Marxism, LGBT depravity, the demonic deception that

Islam is compatible with American culture and values, and every other Luciferian agenda passed off as "compassionate Christianity." Listen to me brethren: find some courage and denounce these people and their heresies because here is the truth of the matter:

- Islam is the military arm of the forces of hell.
- American media is the propaganda arm of the forces of hell.
- Apostate Christianity provides the "religious" covering and immoral framework for the forces of hell.
- The United States Supreme Court has wrested power away from the aristocrats in Congress and has become the legal sledgehammer for the forces of hell.
- Naive, deceived, and compromised Christians are the useful idiots of the forces of hell.
- America's corporations including multi-national companies, central banks, and social media behemoths, provide the financial support for the forces of hell.

There is a reason Jesus confronted the beast religious system of His day: He recognized that it was not of God, did not obey His commands, and was instead worshipping idols of their own creation. The LGBT flag-waving, affirming, proud professing Christians are going to wake up in eternity and experience sheer terror when they hear "depart from Me you workers of iniquity."

Listen to me Christian: there is nothing to be proud of when one man sticks his penis into another man's rectum. Have you lost your mind? That is not love and love has not won anything. Wickedness won and if you can't see that then you are the problem.

The Islamic interfaith dialogue crowd is a picture of what happens when you deny centuries of history, the plain teachings of the Koran, the current speeches of the God-haters scattered all around the world in mosques, and the barbaric atrocities committed daily for Allah's honor. What is there to dialogue about with people who say Jesus Christ was not the Son of God, did not die on a cross, never rose from the dead, and certainly is not the Savior of the world? With the fields white to harvest why are impotent stooges being honored for giving Islamic jihadists cover with their blind ego-driven speeches and seminars?

(4) You will need to realize that not all will follow you. The twelve were amazed but the larger contingency of disciples that followed Jesus was fearful (10:32). As I mentioned above, the twelve were amazed at Jesus' resolve to travel directly to Jerusalem. The twelve knew the heated debates and angry words the religious leaders hurled at Jesus. The twelve had been ridiculed themselves for following Jesus. Watching Jesus walk that road straight into Jerusalem was a lesson they would forget in Gethsemane and in the days following Jesus ascension but, it was also one they remembered and drew strength and courage from after the giving of the Holy Spirit.

Some will fall away because they fear the path you are walking. They fear what they perceive to be the negative consequences for them personally. They will count the cost and decide it is too high a price to pay.

(5) You are going to have to tell people to stop sinning. America is currently in a period of time in which we are witnessing a mass exodus from the church. Do you have any idea why? The reason is simply this: people see very little difference between the lives of professing Christians and the general population. The church does not need another sermon series on being the best parent or spouse you can be. Christians do not need to be told to have their best life now. Christians need to understand that there are answers to their heartbreak. Statistics tell us that pornography is at an all-time high and rising among both men and women who profess faith in Christ. The church doesn't need another sermon series on good sex. It needs clear biblical teaching on the God-given gift of sex that honors each spouse and that brings to bear the spiritual significance of sexual intercourse within marriage. The church needs to recover its identity as the assembly of the saints but it will not until the saints start acting like the people of God once again. The church needs accountability.

Do you want to lead like Jesus? If so then I encourage you to read Mark 10:38. There you see the cost to yourself and all that you count dear in this life. So, ask yourself, are you able to drink the cup Jesus drank? If you want to lead like Jesus, friend, you better buckle up because the ride is going to get bumpy. You are going to be misunderstood and even hated. You will be seen as a threat to the apostates of the beast religious system which is much of American

Christianity, and you will be completely out of step, out of tune, and out of sync with the world system.

Father, I pray that You would raise up men and women who understand the times in which we live and who will not be afraid to lead with fearless conviction and Holy Spirit power, straight into the bared teeth of the Luciferians who control America. Father, equip us with divine courage that we would not flinch at the sight of evil but would instead snarl right back with a ferociousness born of a blood-bought soul. I ask this covering to be upon all who read these words and volunteer to lead like Jesus. In the wonderful, mighty, powerful name of Jesus I ask this, amen!

Chapter Fifteen

Christianity Has Become a Janitorial Service

I was listening to Coach Dave Daubenmire recently and during his Coach Dave Live program he made the point that Christianity as lived out by the overwhelming majority of American Christians has become nothing more than a custodian service. Let that sink in friends. Christians are nothing more than glorified janitors. Ouch! The truth hurts but out of that pain can come an understanding of what needs to change.

How are Christians only glorified janitors? Consider that Christians and the churches they call their spiritual homes spend untold amounts of time, energy, and finances on addiction recovery programs, counseling confused people about marriage, sexuality, interpersonal relationships, parenting, and every sort of life issue imaginable. There is even an army of "life coaches" that offer their services to Christians unable to deal with what their lives have become.

Now some Christians reading this might think, "Well what's wrong with all of those things? Shouldn't Christians be helping people to overcome their problems?" The problem with this strategy, this method of ministry, is that it is reactive instead of proactive. That's right; Christians are reacting to people after the damage has been done. We are like janitors called to clean up the mess Johnnie and Jane make in the classroom because they've never been taught to understand that certain behavior is neither acceptable nor tolerated. A forgotten truth is this: certain behaviors result in negative and often catastrophic consequences for the individual involved and often others as a result of association with or by unfortunate contact with an individual.

Let me give you some concrete examples of what I'm talking about. Here in Ohio where I live, 13% of the state budget is spent on addiction, substance use, and abuse programs.[3] Of the 13%, $0.02 of every budgeted dollar pays for prevention and treatment programs and $0.90 of every budgeted dollar pays for the consequences of addiction, substance use, and abuse. Do those figures suggest anything to you? What they suggest to me is that if we must spend tax payer money on things like this, perhaps the amount spent on prevention should increase so that the amount spent on the consequences can decrease. Does it not follow that more emphasis on prevention might mean

---

[3] Data available by state here
https://www.centeronaddiction.org/addiction/state-spending-addiction-risk-use Accessed August 25, 2018.

less negative consequences and the need for a bloated budget to pay for those consequences?

Further, these negative consequences for certain behavior places a large and growing burden on state health care systems. Consider that:

> The largest share of spending on the consequences of addiction and substance use falls to the health care system. Tobacco, alcohol and drug use cause or contribute to more than 70 other conditions requiring medical care, including cancer, lung disease, heart disease, HIV/AIDS, pregnancy complications, cirrhosis, ulcers and trauma. Nearly 1/3 of all hospital costs are linked to addiction and substance use.[4]

Addiction and substance use and abuse also impacts federal spending related to welfare, mental health, job and family services, and health care. Billions of dollars are authorized annually to assist people with the consequences of their behavior.

Let's now consider the practice of abortion. The absurd ramblings of a demented Chelsea Clinton aside,[5] there is a tremendous toll being paid by Americans today resulting from the now 70 million plus unborn human beings murdered since the Supreme Court invented the "right" to

---

[4] https://www.centeronaddiction.org/policy/costs-of-risky-use-addiction Accessed August 25, 2018.

[5] https://www.cnsnews.com/blog/craig-bannister/chelsea-clinton-roe-helped-add-three-and-half-trillion-dollars-our-economy Accessed August 25, 2018.

murder unborn human beings 45 years ago. This decision by our black-robed despots has had devastating effects.

One of the consequences of the Roe v. Wade invention was Post-Abortion Syndrome. In the early years of abortion women suffered in silence as the effects of their decision to murder their unborn child washed over them like ocean waves. Post-Abortion Syndrome continues to ravage women who undergo an abortion.[6]

The Students for Life organization at the University of Colorado recently published an article titled, "The Cost of Abortion."[7] This short analysis provided several alarming facts. Studies conducted among women who aborted their unborn children revealed:

- 55% expressed guilt.
- 44% complained of nervous disorders.
- 36% reported sleep disorders.
- 31% regretted the decision to abort their unborn child.
- 11% were administered a psychotropic medication by their doctor.

In another study cited that included 500 post-abortion women, 50% admitted to negative emotions concerning their decision to abort their unborn children, and 10% were

---

[6] https://www.lifeissues.org/1996/03/96mar/ Accessed August 25, 2018.
[7] https://www.colorado.edu/studentgroups/studentsforlife/cost.html Accessed August 25 2018.

classified as having developed serious psychiatric problems. Additionally, 30%-50% of post-abortion women reported sexual dysfunction ranging from short to long term beginning immediately after their abortions. The truth of the matter is this: a majority of women who make the decision to abort their unborn children will suffer some type of guilt, shame, sexual dysfunction, and psychiatric trauma, for which a majority will seek medical assistance and prescription drugs to deal with the aforementioned symptoms.

Perhaps even more troubling than the data cited above is the fact that women who abort their unborn children suffer what researchers and medical doctors report as depression often leading to suicide or attempted suicide, and other self-destructive behaviors including drug and alcohol abuse, chronic relationship issues due to dramatic personality changes, an increased tendency toward violence, and difficulty bonding with children they birth after a previous abortion.

Finally, the physical damage done to women who abort their unborn children is suppressed by abortion supporting organizations including hospitals, doctors, medical and psychiatric associations, and research institutions. Researchers not afraid to report what big medicine, big pharma, and big government try to hide, report that upwards of 5% of all women who abort their unborn children suffer sterility as a result of the operation's latent morbidity.[8] Cervical damage almost always occurs and one study reveals that cervical incompetence was found in 75% of women who underwent forced dilation for an abortion.[9] This results in increased risks of miscarriage, premature birth, and complications during later pregnancies. In fact, a major study of first pregnancy abortions reveals that 48% of women who terminated their first pregnancy later experienced on average 2.3 miscarriages for every live birth.[10]

I hope you are still with me. Statistics can be dry and sometimes boring but they serve a purpose. In this instance they serve to vividly illustrate that federal, state, and even local governments are all involved in spending money to address the painful consequences of people's behavior. The church is not immune from this activity either. I see all kinds of churches advertising for clients to attend their programs of recovery from this, that, or the other thing. Pastors get in on the act too. I often see promotions on social media about a "new and dynamic series that will teach you how to avoid the pitfalls of (you fill in the blank)."

I'm all for helping people in their time of need with few qualifications. But the idea that the church, that Christians, should be running around taking care of all the foolish people that believe they can engage in behavior that they

---

[8] http://afterabortion.org/1990/abortion-complications/ Accessed August 25, 2018
[9] ibid.
[10] ibid.

know will lead them into a dark and difficult place, is naïve and misguided to say the least.

Instead of spending all our time putting band aids on gaping wounds that require surgery and stiches, how about we go straight to the source of the behavior that causes these painful consequences and eliminate them?

Listen folks, Satan is a liar and always has been. The lies he hisses in people's ears need rebuked. Alcohol is dangerous. I'm not suggesting you become a teetotaler but I am saying you better be very careful with your use of alcohol. It might take you places you never intended to go and demand from you things you are not willing to forfeit. Alcohol is a cruel master that cares nothing about the things you do. If you allow yourself to become controlled by it you will lose everything you hold dear. If you think you are the one person that can beat the odds then you are more foolish than you realize.

In light of the tremendous drug and alcohol addiction crisis we face as Americans, it is very troubling that the so-called hipster Christians, you know, the skinny jeans, bearded, beer drinking, pot smoking, "new Christianity" Christians, engage in these addictive behaviors. Listen folks the church is supposed to reflect Christ not the culture.

If Christians really want to help drug and alcohol addicts then maybe we should start going to places that sell the stuff, like say, bars or night clubs, and stand outside with signs that suggest what they are about to do will destroy their lives and then engage them in conversation. If we can save anyone from the hell-hole of addiction don't you think it is worth our time? Let's go to the source before the mess is made!

If the church really wants to help victims of the modern day demonic ritual of child sacrifice euphemistically called abortion "choice" then it should be marching in front of abortion clinics in their communities. Christians should be shouting from the rooftops that aborting unborn children is indeed murder. Stop believing that satanic lie that "if you tell people that abortion is murder they will just tune you out as some type of radical." If you don't tell them abortion is murder you'll answer to your Creator as to why you didn't tell them the truth. Here's the truth folks: holding signs showing the dismembered bodies of unborn children is an undeniable truth that abortion is murder. That's why so many people will not look at a sign like that. But when someone does and it causes them to pause and think, don't you think that is worth your time to engage them in conversation about the precious gift of life?

Think of this folks: if you go to an abortion clinic and persuade one woman to change her mind you have saved her from the likelihood of serious future psychological and medical issues AND saved her unborn child from the executioner's forceps. Let's not stop there though. If we are going to persuade women to not murder their unborn children we better be prepared to help those women to find a good home for their child should they decide to allow someone else to adopt. Wouldn't that be a better way for a church to spend its resources than on a new bigger or better building?

Pastor's how about you start preaching on the sanctity of life every Sunday? Life is precious in God's eyes so let's remind people to stop viewing pornography. It destroys the mind and devalues people, making the joy of sexual intimacy a vapor that disappears.

Christians if we want to graduate from being janitors that clean up the mess people make of their lives then let's get proactive in our churches, in our communities, in our families, and in every other thing we are involved in. Let's take the fight to the enemy by reclaiming our streets.

Chapter Sixteen

Cruise Ships and Troop Carriers

Let me define the term pastor for you.

- Do you lead a home Bible study with your family? If so you are a shepherd to them. MEN YOU MUST BE A SHEPHERD TO YOUR FAMILY AS PART OF YOUR GOD ORDAINED ROLE.
- Do you lead a Bible study for some of your co-workers and neighbors? Then you are a shepherd to them.
- Do you lead a Bible study at the local assembly you attend? Then you are a shepherd to them.
- Do you have an online ministry of Bible teaching that is effectively discipling other believers? Then you are a shepherd to them.

This is not about ordination. Here's the only ordination God is interested in – do you have His Holy Spirit living within you and do you love God and God's people? If you answered yes them you have a divine ordination on you to continue to shepherd God's people.

Now, let's have a family chat. It's time for some straight talk. The globalists, corporatists, and the Luciferians running our print & electronic media including our social media are coming after true believers. They are being aided and abetted by our government which is no friend to born-again believers. Let me show you what happens when citizens cede too much power to their government.

Example - *Patriot* movie clip – "A Shepherd must tend the flock and at times fight off the wolves." I'm a pastor with a pastor's heart for God's people. In my opinion, pastors should be leading the charge in this fight!

Example - Benjamin Franklin quote:

> "We must, indeed, all hang together or, most assuredly, we shall all hang separately."

Friends, the true Church of Jesus Christ cannot be conquered BUT it is being attacked today. The body of Christ is under a most ferocious assault.

Sadly, much of the visible Church is ill-prepared for what is happening. In fact much of the visible, organized, brick-and-mortar Church is compromised today and there is no fight in them.

There is a reason for the apostasy we see all around us. Let me illustrate what I believe the reason is with a couple of video clips. I'll be asking which one of these two clips best represents the Church today.

Much of the Church in America thinks the Christian faith is like a cruise ship sailing through the sunshine without a care. Their thinking is "we're just going to sail along on smooth seas until Jesus comes back to rescue us to the big cruise liner in the sky." Remember the lyrics to the Love Boat TV show? "The Love Boat promises something for everyone." That sounds exactly like the Laodicean church of today.

- "Come to our services – no one will ever be offended here." "We're inclusive!" There should be a skull and cross bones on those church buildings to warn anyone thinking of entering that they do so at their own spiritual peril.

There are lots of so-called pastors and various ministries that are willing to continue to teach this narrative of "something for everyone." There's big money in "Love Boat Christianity." However, this is the "peace and safety" message disguised as modern man's redefined tolerance and it is a deadly virus.

We know what the Bible says about that don't we? Sudden destruction will come upon them.

Now let's look at how the Bible really describes the Church in my opinion: In Saving Private Ryan – "What do we do now sir?" Much of the Church today is shell-shocked and immobilized by fear. American culture has seemingly spun out of control and there are shots being fired at Christianity from every direction.

- Captain Miller's instructions in Saving Private Ryan? "Head for the sea wall." That is interesting for two reasons: (1) in order to get to the sea wall they had to run directly into the enemy's fire. (2) the sea wall was the last obstacle that separated them from the enemy. Overcome the sea wall and you will meet the enemy face to face.

Now, here's my point friends – our perspective on who we are as the body of Christ will result in specific and identifiable characteristics. The wrong perspective will result in the wrong actions AND it will require scripture twisting and heterodoxy to support. BUT the right perspective will enlighten your understanding and you will acquire the mind of Christ and rightly understand our duty to God.

From the Love Boat and Saving Private Ryan alone we learn at least 4 things:

- The Christian life is not about having your best life now. Things will not always work out as you planned.
- The Church should never be making promises to anyone of anything that is not scripturally rooted and we better be sure to tell people the whole Gospel story.
- True Christians run to the battle not away from it.

- You cannot engage the enemy until you overcome the obstacles that he places in your path. Our enemy will hide behind sea walls not expecting you to storm them with Holy Spirit empowered courage and vigor.

Note-takers – if we rightly understand that the Church is a troop carrier then in the least, these 3 things will follow.

- Our behavior will be much different than those Christians who believe they are on the Love Boat.
- Our use of God's resources will be much different than Love Boat Christians.
- AND, our sense of urgency will be much more pronounced than the Love Boat crowd.

The delusion that has gripped much of the visible, organized, brick-and-mortar Church – what I call the Love Boat crowd is rooted in theology misinformed by modern day philosophical and ideological confusion.

The Church has been hamstrung by erroneous theology. (No I'm not talking about eschatology – especially your view of the rapture. Stop attacking each other over when Christ is going to return and receive His body unto Himself.) WHAT WE DON'T NEED TO SEE ANY MORE IS A CIRCLE FIRING SQUAD WHERE WE'RE SHOOTING EACH OTHER.

Here's the fake/false/abhorrent theology that I believe is at the root of the Love Boat deception – a large number of Christians have become convinced that our assignment on this earth is to clean it up and make it ready for Christ's return.

In other words they believe that they can create a new Eden right here if they just love people. They would not describe their thinking that way, but it is true nevertheless.

The issue is simply this – we cannot reconcile a fallen, sinful world with any form of utopianism, Christian or otherwise! We are not told to make this world a better, happier, place outside of the transforming power of the Gospel that changes hearts and minds. We are not bringing the Kingdom of God here by loving people. Christ will establish His Kingdom when He returns.

NOW LET ME STARTLE SOME OF YOU - You cannot love people into salvation folks. Salvation is free to all who humbly confess their sin and repent of it, trusting in the finished work of Jesus Christ for their complete cleansing and forgiveness. The mercy of God falls upon all those who are willing to receive it by God's prescribed manner. Salvation is solely a work of the Holy Spirit.

If you think, "well Mike, I'm just going to love people because if I just love people eventually they will see their error and repent," then let me ask you to do something - STOP IT! Love people certainly, but do not for one second think that you can somehow love them right into salvation.

Our assignment is not to turn this world into a Christian theme park of sunshine and lollipops. The goal of our faith is:

- To magnify the Lord Jesus Christ in our words and deeds.
- To tell others about the salvation the Father offers through faith in Jesus the Son.
- It is to warn them of the coming judgment of God upon all those who reject the Son as the only means of eternal life with God.

Now, what that means in this fallen world is we are on a mission to save Private Ryan! But don't think that the enemy of our souls is going to let you parade around sharing your faith and saving every Private Ryan you meet. Our enemy is going to be shooting at you from entrenched positions every time you come into his crosshairs.

BUT - the true Church, brothers and sisters, is a Holy Spirit empowered Search & Rescue team. We, the remnant, are the special forces of God's army. We are the scouts out reconnoitering the land, looking for survivors and engaging the enemy with deadly force.

We are quite simply, and need to see ourselves as, the last hurdle the enemy must leap before he drags a soul to hell. Our assignment is to be that obstacle that the enemy cannot scale, that fortress that the enemy cannot breach, that son or daughter of God that stands firmly upon the rock that is Jesus Christ!

Singer and songwriter Steve Camp, now Pastor Steve Camp, wrote a song several years ago called "Run to the Battle." Here are some of the lyrics:

> *Some people want to live within the sound of chapel bells*
> *But I want to run a mission, a yard from the gate of hell*
> *And with everyone you meet, take them the gospel and share it well*
> *Look around you as you hesitate, another soul just fell*
> *Let's run to the battle*

We used to sing a hymn back in the day titled "Rescue the Perishing." Here's what verses 1 and 4 say.

Verse One:
Rescue the perishing, care for the dying,
Snatch them in pity from sin and the grave;
Weep o'er the erring one, lift up the fallen,
Tell them of Jesus, the mighty to save.

Verse Four:

Rescue the perishing, duty demands it;
Strength for thy labor the Lord will provide;
Back to the narrow way patiently win them;
Tell the poor wand'rer a Savior has died.

What has changed today? For one when we sing that hymn we don't need to look outside the Church. We only need look to our right and left to see people that need rescued by the true Gospel of salvation through faith in Christ alone.

Now some people might be thinking, "wow that's a harsh statement Mike." Let me remind you of what Jesus said in Matthew 13:24-30

> *"Jesus presented another parable to them, saying, "The kingdom of heaven may be compared to a man who sowed good seed in his field. ²⁵ But while his men were sleeping, his enemy came and sowed tares among the wheat, and went away. ²⁶ But when the wheat sprouted and bore grain, then the tares became evident also. ²⁷ The slaves of the landowner came and said to him, 'Sir, did you not sow good seed in your field? How then does it have tares?' ²⁸ And he said to them, 'An enemy has done this!' The slaves *said to him, 'Do you want us, then, to go and gather them up?' ²⁹ But he *said, 'No; for while you are gathering up the tares, you may uproot the wheat with them. ³⁰ Allow both to grow together until the harvest; and in the time of the harvest I will say to the reapers, "First gather up the tares and bind them in bundles to burn them up; but gather the wheat into my barn."*

Brothers and sisters, much of the visible, organized Church has become a tare-infested field.

True Christians are involved in a conflict, a spiritual war for the souls of people and we don't have to look far to find them. Churches are filled with them.

IF we come to grips with this reality then that should change our behavior. Our demeanor should reflect the gravity of what we know to be true.

We are called to be sober minded, alert, and fully armed. This is what the Apostle Paul said in Ephesians 6:11-13

> [11] *Put on the full armor of God, so that you will be able to stand firm against the schemes of the devil.* [12] *For our struggle is not against flesh and blood, but against the rulers, against the powers, against the world forces of this darkness, against the spiritual forces of wickedness in the heavenly places.* [13] *Therefore, take up the full armor of God, so that you will be able to resist in the evil day, and having done everything, to stand firm.*

How many times have you heard this passage quoted and taught? Several times right?

Do you realize that there is a huge difference between hearing the truth and knowing the truth? Here's what Jesus said in Matthew 13:30-32

> [30] *As He spoke these things, many came to believe in Him.* [31] *So Jesus was saying to those Jews who had believed Him, "If you continue in My word, then you are truly disciples of Mine;* [32] *and you will know the truth, and the truth will make you free."*

So Jesus says that abiding in His word – that means obeying and trusting – is the mark of a true disciple.

But abiding is an action word. So let's take this a step farther. Do you understand that there is a difference between knowing truth and living the truth?

In other words, living the truth, or abiding in the truth is the expectation of all disciples of Jesus Christ.

Those who claim to know the truth of who Jesus is, but refuse to live that truth in obedience to Him are in the least practical atheists and worst case scenario, false converts.

So again, there is a war going on, and if we believe that, then our lives will reflect that belief. Our behavior will be drastically different from the world we live in. We will live sober lives for our King!

- In my years in the military I never once witnessed a flippant attitude from anyone when we were out on patrol. Every single man was focused, alert, listening, and ready to take action. You know why? Because our lives were dependent on each other being ready to act.
- Are we ready to act?

Now for the 2nd point - When this is our demeanor – when we are trained and ready to act - we will use the resources God has given us wisely. Folks it is time to invest more wisely in the Kingdom of God.

Look around this room. Look at all the ministries represented here. Let me encourage you to prayerfully consider how best to use the resources God has entrusted to you.

Our assignment is to save the Private Ryan's wherever we meet them and to push back against the darkness. IF you are attending meetings with a local body of Christ and you are not growing in your faith then let me ask you to do a couple of things.

- Determine what it is that is lacking. Is there clear and accurate Bible teaching being consistently presented? Is there ministry to the body? Is there outreach to the lost? ARE YOU involved in any of those things? Determine what if anything is lacking and then approach your pastor and have a conversation about standing in the gap.
- If you do that and you are told that nothing is going to change, I suggest you find another body of believers to grow with and to minister to.

Consider this principle friends: we criticize our government for attempting to solve problems with our tax dollars, throwing good money down a black hole from which we never see any beneficial results.

The remnant body of Christ needs to be wise, about how we invest our resources too. Stop investing in Love Boat Christianity. Perhaps consider one of the many ministries represented here today.

Then, finally brothers and sisters, our sense of urgency will be a driving force in our lives. Our behavior will be much different, how we use our resources will be much different, and our sense of urgency will be much different.

We will understand the times that we live in, and what we need to be doing. I'm reminded often of a situation that Pastor Chuck Smith talked about in the very early days of the Jesus People Movement and Calvary Chapel in the mid to late 1960s and early 1970s.

- Pastor Chuck went to the beaches of Southern California to talk to the hippies and surfers about salvation in Jesus Christ.
- When they started getting saved and coming to the body of believers that Chuck pastored, people started complaining because they had just put new carpet in the building and all those barefooted hippies and surfers were walking in with filthy feet and leaving dirt and sand everywhere.
- So some of the elders came to Pastor Chuck and said "we need to do something about this." Chuck agreed and said, "You are right we do. Rip out all that new carpet so we don't have to worry about it."

You know what folks? The problem was solved immediately. No more complaining about dirty carpet or feet.

Here's my point friends – we simply must root out any attitude that causes us to look down our noses at lost people no matter how filthy their feet might be.

The Apostle Paul said this to the Corinthian believers in 1 Corinthians 6:11

> *[11] Such were some of you; but you were washed, but you were sanctified, but you were justified in the name of the Lord Jesus Christ and in the Spirit of our God.*

What were the "such were some of you" characteristics? Here's what Paul mentions – fornicators, idolaters, adulterers, effeminate, homosexuals, thieves, covetous, drunkards, revilers, and swindlers (1 Corinthians 6:9-10).

Let me be very clear about something here friends. I'm not talking about accepting sin. I'm talking about helping people to overcome the sin that entangles them by preaching Jesus and then putting arms and feet to the Gospel by assisting them in overcoming their struggles.

And this is a real battle. Consider what the writer to the Hebrews stated in Hebrews 12:1-3

> *[1] Therefore, since we have so great a cloud of witnesses surrounding us, let us also lay aside every encumbrance and*

the sin which so easily entangles us, and let us run with endurance the race that is set before us, ² fixing our eyes on Jesus, the author and perfecter of faith, who for the joy set before Him endured the cross, despising the shame, and has sat down at the right hand of the throne of God. ³ For consider Him who has endured such hostility by sinners against Himself, so that you will not grow weary and lose heart.

The Apostle Peter reminds us in 1 Peter 2:11

11Beloved, I urge you as aliens and strangers to abstain from fleshly lusts which wage war against the soul.

And Jude says in Jude 3

3Beloved, while I was making every effort to write you about our common salvation, I felt the necessity to write to you appealing that you contend earnestly for the faith which was once for all handed down to the saints.

Friends, it saddens me to say that much of the visible, organized Church is compromised. They are focused on everything except what matters most – preaching Jesus Christ, and rescuing the perishing, which includes the most vulnerable among us – the unborn children of America suffering through a modern day satanic holocaust.

I see other Christians circling the wagons to keep the world out. Friends, I don't see a circling the wagons strategy in the Bible. I tell you what I do see. I see a Saving Private

Ryan strategy that involves getting on the troop carriers which is the remnant body of Christ and taking the fight to the enemy by storming the beaches of Satan's strongholds.

And let me remind you of this brethren. Our hope is not in Washington DC. We are not called to make a political, economic, or social utopia by collaborating with the enemy!

Let's determine today in this place, that we will no longer tolerate worldly Love Boat Christianity and that prevailing attitude and behavior among those who profess Jesus Christ.

Instead, let us determine today as God is our witness, to throw off the shackles of complacency, and engage in this war against our great God and His people.

I remind you of these words spoken so eloquently by the actress in the Patriot movie clip: Will you now when you are needed most, stop at only words?"

Chapter Seventeen

What's Love Got To Do With It?

It's physical, only logical; you must try to ignore, that it means more than that.[11]

I was speaking at a local fellowship recently as a part of their twentieth anniversary celebration. It is good to look back and be reminded of God's faithfulness toward us. Often we only see His guiding hand in retrospect. One of the points I stressed to those in attendance was the need to couple perseverance with faithfulness to God.

Perseverance is an admirable quality but without faithfulness to God it is really meaningless. People persevere in the wrong things all the time. Faithfulness to God makes perseverance meaningful.

Faithfulness to God includes faithfulness to His revealed word to us. That means that we study the Bible to

---

[11] Tina Turner, *What's Love Got To Do With It?,* from the album "Private Dancer" released in 1984. Lyrics written by Terry Britten and Graham Lyle.

understand what God has said and then we order our lives accordingly. This is a straight forward truth with no ambiguity. Psalm 119:4 makes this clear: "Thou hast ordained Thy precepts, that we should keep them diligently."[12]

The temptation is to order our lives according to what is convenient for us. Sometimes personal comfort is a factor. People naturally resist making decisions and taking public stands on issues that they perceive as "out of step" with their social context for fear of rebuttal, rebuke, or loss of esteem among their peers. Other times the pressure of wanting to maintain a friendship or other relationship becomes of primary concern. Regardless of the reason, when Christians deviate from the clear teaching of the Bible they are compromising their faith and bringing reproach to God's name among the heathen. King David knew this well from experience. He cried out to God, "May those who wait for Thee not be ashamed through me, O Lord God of hosts; May those who seek Thee not be dishonored through me, O God of Israel" (Psalm 69:6 NASB).

Mankind has already experienced the violent and devastating consequences of abandoning God's word for what is convenient. It was the serpent who suggested to Eve that there was wiggle room in the interpretation and certainly the application of God's commands. "Has God

---

[12] Unless otherwise stated, all Scripture quotations are taken from The New American Standard Bible, (La Habra, CA: Lockman Foundation, 1978).

said?" was meant to cause Eve to questioned God's integrity and His love for her. A good and loving God wouldn't withhold anything from His creation if they earnestly desire it would He? That was the seed of doubt Satan planted in Eve's mind that led to confusion that resulted in a tragic choice to disobey the clear command of God.

After the fiery dart of doubt that Satan delivered found Eve's heart, she took a second look at the tree and "saw that the tree was good for food, and that it was a delight to the eyes, and that the tree was desirable to make one wise, she took from its fruit and ate; and she gave also to her husband with her, and he ate" (Genesis 3:6). This is the consequence of denying the clear teaching of God's word: you will make decisions that you see as personally beneficial for any number of reasons, with little to no thought of the consequences for yourself or others. It is an act of presuming upon the love of God and expecting Him to understand.

WHAT'S LOVE GOT TO DO WITH IT?

Several factors have come together over a short period of time that has impacted the church negatively. One factor is the abandonment of the teaching of the word of God. Many pastors have simply stopped teaching the Bible. Instead they teach pop-psychology, new age universalism, and hobby-horse themed series that they believe help people "where they are." Far too many pastors now determine the course of the church's teaching, education, and equipping ministries based on the "felt needs" of congregants.

What do the felt needs of people have to do with teaching them what the Bible says? How has this strategy of appealing to people's flesh come to pass as an equivalent for expounding the Scriptures? Why are pastors fashioning their teaching ministries based on what they are convinced people need in the emotional and/or psychological realm?

I believe pastors do this for very simple reasons. First, pastors think if they appeal to things that interest people then they will become engaged in his and the church's ministry. They will "feel" invested and will then be more likely to participate in other things. Second, telling people what they want to hear or believe they need to hear, keeps them coming back and when people come back then the opportunity for the financing of other church ministries is increased. Third, and the most serious error pastors make is to believe that attempting to address people's felt needs is actually ministry to them. But, in the process of employing these strategies pastors abandon the clear teaching of the Scriptures on nearly every subject. This last issue is really the crux of the matter. Pastors have lost faith in the Bible. Pastors do not trust the Word of God any longer. The Bible is seen more as a launching point that gives a cover of propriety for the most egregious anti-God and certainly anti-biblical nonsense the church has ever witnessed.

The basis for this mass confusion in the pulpits of America is that pastors are not teaching truth but appealing to experience. What I mean by that is pastors have fallen prey to the ubiquitous fog of postmodernism. Truth as proposition, truth as something that can be known, as something that is unchanging regardless of the time, place, or people has been completely abandoned. Experience as subjective truth has triumphed over objective truth in American pulpits.

Pastors have adopted the strategies mentioned above in spite of the many exhortations, admonishments, encouragements, and warnings against abandoning the Bible. Consequently many people who profess faith in Jesus Christ have given up living by the truths, statutes, laws, and precepts of God. Their reasoning is that if the pastor doesn't think it is important then they shouldn't either. What's really important, they are told, is to know how much God loves them. Pastors are quick to assure their congregants that God desires that they live a happy, well-adjusted life.

Much of the American church today is totally absorbed with a form of therapeutic deism. God has become a "god of my needs." He is taken down from the shelf when there is a need and replaced when the crisis passes. The Israelites were judged severely for their idolatry. Will American Christians escape the same consequence for their idolatry?

"But God loves me so much that He wants me to be happy." Is that the love of God? Is God's focus, His ultimate desire for us, that we be happy? Examining much of the landscape of Christendom today gives that impression. The central message of the church in America today is the love of God. His love is best illustrated people are told, in His desire that they be happy. Thus, whatever makes someone happy must be the will of God for them. Let's follow that demonic logic to its rotten conclusion.

LOVE HAS NOTHING TO DO WITH IT

One of several hot button issues in our culture today is homosexuality. The agenda of the LGBT movement has been for many years, the normalization of their sexual depravity. They have been successful in this effort. In American secular culture it is an unquestioned belief that a man sticking his penis into another man's rectum is love.

Does that statement shock you? Do you want to stop reading now? Was your first thought after reading that truth, "I can't believe he just said that"? If that is you then you are a victim of the secular propaganda machine and perhaps you've just now come to realize that. Your shock over the truth of what sex between two men consists of is proof you have become normalized to the euphemisms the homosexuals and their allies in the church use to cloak the depravity of their actions.

What do I mean by that? Simply this: if speaking the truth about what homosexuality is shocks you then you have accepted the lie that homosexuality is love and whatever is of love is alright between consenting adults.

The current state of affairs within much of the church reveals a capitulation to the strategies of the enemy of our souls. Homosexuality and same-sex union affirming Christians have been at the forefront of propagandizing Christian youth. Millennials have been specifically targeted and the results are gut-wrenching.

One strategy utilized by those inside of and associated with Revoice, the Southern Baptist ERLC, The Gospel Coalition, The Southern Baptist Theological Seminary, Covenant Seminary, and now LOVEboldly, is the idea of friendship. The most common response I have heard from Christians who think homosexuality is just a "preference" is this: "Well, I have lots of friends who are gay and I love them so I support their position."

The organizations and its members listed above are using this emotion, this postmodern, experience based propaganda to drive a wedge between people and the truth of God's Word. By doing so they are aiding and abetting the destruction of the foundations of evangelicalism. Their goal is clearly to usher in a form cultural Marxism. Perhaps they think that by being involved in leading many into apostasy they can step out of and avoid the war against Christianity. To those individuals I commend the words of Mordecai to Esther: Do not think you can avoid destruction. Indeed, you better pray you do not avoid the same consequence you are enabling because if you do, you are part of the end times one world beast religious system and you have a much bigger problem.

Do you understand what has happened to these people? They have become disciples of postmodernism, in which feelings trump everything else. What people feel is now the barometer of truth. Christians have adopted the world's way of thinking. "My friend has these feelings and I love my friend so I think his feelings are right." Never mind that Christians are warned not to trust our feelings because they can lead you into wickedness (Jeremiah 17:9).

The Scripture says that friendship with the world makes us enemies of God (James 4:4). Some might object, saying that this is speaking of the world's system, the philosophies of the world system. My response is that this way of thinking is adopted by people and their worldview governs the lenses through which they make decisions. Even then, Paul writes that we are to destroy every speculation and idea that raises itself up against the knowledge of God (2 Corinthians 10:5). Additionally, Paul had this to say to those who think they can remain in their sin because God loves me as they are:

> Or do you not know that the unrighteous will not inherit the kingdom of God? Do not be deceived; neither fornicators, nor idolaters, nor adulterers, nor effeminate, nor homosexuals, nor thieves, nor *the* covetous, nor drunkards, nor revilers, nor swindlers, will inherit the kingdom of God. Such were some of you; but you were washed, but you were sanctified, but you were justified in the name of

the Lord Jesus Christ and in the Spirit of our God.[13]

PERSEVERE THROUGH FAITHFULNESS

I remember singing an old hymn long ago. *I Have Decided to Follow Jesus* was sung during invitations in the Baptist church I attended as a young man. The lyrics said in part: "Though none go with me still I will follow." The implication is that following Jesus will cost you something. 1 Corinthians 15:33 says: "Do not be deceived: Bad company corrupts good morals." Sometimes the price we pay to follow Jesus is giving up friendship with people who insist that Jesus loves them and accepts them even when they are living in blatant sin. Such is the case with those who insist their homosexuality is consistent with Christian faith. It is likely the case that your continued friendship with people who refuse to give up their sin is a sign that you have been compromised. Paul's instructions to the Corinthian believers is appropriate to remember here: "Do not be bound together with unbelievers; for what partnership has righteousness and lawlessness, or what fellowship has light with darkness? Or what harmony has Christ with Belial, or what has a believer in common with an unbeliever?" (2 Corinthians 6:14-15).

Even though I understand that people who insist on engaging in homosexual behavior do not believe the Bible's instructions, I give them nonetheless. Even though I have heard many professing Christians say that they support

---

[13] 1 Corinthians 6:9-11

homosexual behavior because they have friends who are homosexual, I challenge them to reconsider that position. Recall these words of Jesus as you choose this day whom you will serve:

> *"He who loves father or mother more than Me is not worthy of Me; and he who loves son or daughter more than Me is not worthy of Me. And he who does not take his cross and follow after Me is not worthy of Me. He who has found his life will lose it, and he who has lost his life for My sake will find it"* **(Matthew 10:37-39).**

Christian, if you are one of those individuals who is loving your homosexual friend straight to hell by not telling them the truth, I call you to forsake that and return to serving Jesus with your whole heart. What's love got to do with it? Short answer: everything. True love is from God, and He loves us with an untainted love that desires to see us walk in holiness before Him. When we adopt the world's way of thinking concerning what constitutes love, we are ignoring what God says about the subject. His is the definitive answer concerning all things.

What we need today are pastors who will obey the LORD in all things and live, preach, and teach His instructions. Through the prophet Ezekiel God said He wants pastors who will teach His people the difference between the holy and the profane, and cause them to discern between the unclean and the clean" (Ezekiel 44:23). Is God's desire for His people any less today?

Chapter Eighteen

The Deep State Revealed Biblically

One of my greatest joys in life is to teach the Bible. Any day and time is always a good time to open up the Bible and hear what God wants to say to us today. That is because Scripture is relevant for every day and age.

Lately I have had an increasing opportunity to discuss events we are witnessing in America and around the world with many people. I see this as a great blessing from God and also as a responsibility that I do not take lightly.

Most Americans are troubled and frustrated by the violence of the Progressive Marxist Leftists and their allies. The demonic insanity of the Maxine Waters wing of the Left is alarming. Equally troubling is the rise of Islamic politicians who unashamedly advocate for Sharia Law in America. It seems that what Louis Farrakhan and Linda Sarsour dream of is gaining momentum across this nation.

Some people are shocked at what they perceive to be the

sudden shift in American values. However, the illustration of the frog in the kettle is an apt representation of the last fifty plus years. While Americans slept the enemy infiltrated our communities, our schools, and our governments at every level. The Church didn't see it happening and those appointed to be Watchmen did not warn of the enemy's advancement. The kettle is now boiling and the frogs are the main course. In case there is any doubt as to who the frogs are friends, they are you and I who hold a viewpoint that America will never be great again unless we return to our Christian heritage and to the rule of Constitutional Law under which our republic can thrive once again.

The Bible serves as a remarkable reminder that there is nothing new under the sun. One of the most often asked questions is "What is wrong with America and the world today?" This type of question is almost always followed by "What can we do to change things?"

Friends, what is wrong with America and indeed the world, is that certain men have creeped in with a lust for power and control. The power these people wield is of demonic origin. These people are known collectively by various names but the current name of choice is the Deep State, and it is clearly revealed in the Bible. We see it in Psalm 2. In 12 short verses, the psalmist succinctly describes a timeless truth. That truth is this: when people abandon God terrible things happen. When standards of right and wrong are constructed and enforced by those with a lust for power and control people will suffer on a global scale.

Please understand this: the machinations of the anti-American God-haters in our midst are in-tune with and directed by the globalists who desire to bring America under their control. Some would argue that America is already controlled by an unelected, unseen cabal. I would not argue against that perspective. However, they do not have complete control yet.

Let's examine the remedy for turning back the Deep State. Note Psalm 2:1 which reads in the New American Standard translation: "Why are the nations in an uproar and the people devising a vain thing?" The King James Version says: "Why do the heathen rage and the people imagine a vain thing?"

The root word for uproar and rage comes from a word that describes the snorting of a war horse who knows a battle is looming and is working itself into a froth. So the nations are roaring or in an uproar at a frenzied pitch. They are snorting and stomping their feet and making quite a demonstration. This sounds like Black Lives Matter, Antifa, La Raza, Nation of Islam, Council for American - Islamic Relations, and every other anti-American, anti-freedom, anti-liberty, anti-God organization that the propaganda arm of the globalists – the American main stream media – admires, promotes, and covers up their atrocities. Clearly something has agitated these foot soldiers of hell.

In Psalm 2:2 we read that the leaders of the nations that are in an uproar, the kings and rulers, have taken counsel together. That means that the leaders of the nations have strategized and coordinated a plan of attack against the source of their frustration and agitation. We don't have to guess who or what the source is because in verse 2 we read that it is the LORD and His Anointed. LORD is Yahweh – The Father - and His Anointed is Jesus Christ.

Notice in verse 3 the reason for this rebellion against God the Father and Jesus the Son: the refusal of the nations to submit to the rule of God. "Let us tear their fetters apart and cast away their cords from us."

Friends what we are seeing here is the rebel heart that refuses to bow the knee and submit to God's loving rule. This is the result of sin. Human nature is predisposed against God. That is the doctrine of original sin. The nature of sin is deception and delusion. Sin creates in the heart of every rebel an arrogance that makes them believe they can reject God without consequence.

Note back in verse 1 the psalmist asks why the people are devising a vain thing. That vain thing is imagining that they can throw off God's moral law, His righteous rule, and be better off for it.

The world as a whole has embraced this idea that each individual and groups of individuals that together form communities and nations can be moral "Sampsons." People have imagined the arrogant and vain thing that they have the power and ability to throw off the moral fetters of God's wisdom and love, that they have the power to resist God and create for themselves a utopian paradise where

God is not necessary, and that they can do this without any consequences. Doesn't that describe America and the world today? It certainly describes every attempt at a communist/socialist utopia that has without exception turned into a nightmare for the people of every nation that has tried it.

We have witnessed this very thing in America. Our enlightened judges have created rights out of thin air and have purposely refashioned America into their debauched vision. Consider for example these court cases and the results.

- 1962 Engel vs. Vitale resulted in the removal of prayer from public schools.
- 1963 Abington School District vs. Schempp resulted in the removal of Bible reading from public schools.
- 1973 Rowe vs. Wade ruled abortion a constitutional right and has resulted in the murder of over 50 million unborn children.
- 1980 Sone vs. Graham removed the Ten Commandments from public schools and government buildings.
- 2013 United States vs. Windsor nullified the Defense of Marriage Act (DOMA).
- 2015 Obergefell vs. Hodges ruled sodomite unions legal across America.

What verse 3 really says is "Let us be free to commit every kind of sin our minds can imagine. Let us be our own judges, let us be our own gods. We do not need God."

A nation that has gleefully murdered 70 million and counting preborn human beings, that celebrates the pride of unconscionable sexual deviancy, that teaches children they can choose which gender they want to be, that sells human beings for the fulfillment of the sexual fantasies of those willing to pay for them, and who tells its citizens that it must continue to finance an out of control oligarchy called the US Federal Government is ripe for judgment.

The so-called freedom those who oppose God are choosing for themselves is not freedom at all. It is instead bondage wrapped in a satanic bow. The devil always collects on his contracts.

The enemy of God and His people is Satan and he is the father of lies who seeks to kill and destroy all that God has created. Freedom from God results in an eternity free from Him as well. That friend is hell.

What is God's response to this rebellion? We see two separate responses in Psalm 2. The first response is seen in verses 4-5. God laughs derisively, mocks, and scorns the pitiful state of these rebels. God is not wringing His hands in heaven trying to figure out what to do or how to make people love and obey Him.

Westernized American Christianity has downplayed the fact that God is a holy and righteous judge who will respond in wrath and fury toward all those who reject Him. The Church has aided and abetted this false teaching that God is the great benevolent benefactor in the sky and eventually all people will see the light and acknowledge Him.

Sadly many Christians have adopted this pseudo-gospel message that elevates God's mercy, grace, and forgiveness while simultaneously minimizing the need for people to repent and confess their sins.

The second response God gives to rebels is to offer a provision for the forgiveness of sins and a way of reconciliation with Him. That is verses 6-9.Take note of these points:

- God offers the rebel nations and people a King of His choosing in verse 6 – "I have installed my King." That King is Jesus.
- This was made sure as a testimony from God in the life, death, and resurrection of Jesus – verse 7 is quoted in Acts 13:33 as prophecy fulfilled.
- In verse 8 we see that God offers redemption and reconciliation through King Jesus. This leads to a life of discipleship. We become prized possessions and the inheritance of Jesus.
- Rejecting God and His offer of salvation through faith in Jesus Christ results in judgment. Verse 9 says Christ will break the nations with a rod of iron and shatter them like earthenware.

With this information in hand God calls the kings of the earth to make a decision. When God is rightly understood, when His moral laws are grasped and viewed in light of His character, people are accountable to make a decision concerning who He is and who Jesus Christ the Son is.

This is what we see in verses 10-12. Note the following points:

- End your rebellion. Show wisdom and discernment in recognizing God; not vanity in rejecting Him (v10; v1).
- Give God praise, glory, honor by repenting, believing, honoring and receiving (v11).
- Understand that there is salvation is no one else but Jesus Christ the Son (v12). "Do homage to the Son."
- Receive assurance of your salvation (v12) – "How blessed are all those who take refuge in Him."

I hope that you see the value of using Psalm 2 to speak with people about what we see happening in America and the world today. It is a timeless reminder of God's principles for living life as His creation.

Let me offer a summary and conclusion to the original questions many people ask today. What is wrong with the world? Simply put friends, the world is reaping a whirlwind of consequences by rejecting God. When God's moral law is not upheld then every individual is free to construct their own morality and the result is chaos and ultimately tyranny as the more ruthless among the world's people gain power and control.

America and the world are teetering on the edge of financial, political, and social collapse on many different fronts. Hostilities are increasing around the world. How much longer can the world keep from falling headlong into a major world-engulfing conflict?

The vain imaginings of people are increasingly debased and harmful to mind and body. The depraved insistence that Americans celebrate men who want to believe they are women, men who want to be recognized as married to other men, and the gutting of our social fabric through the public schools indoctrination program has left America confused and bewildered.

What can we do? As Psalm 2 points out, the remedy to the chaos, confusion, and calamity that has fallen upon America and indeed the world is to bow the knee to God, confess our sins, repent of our forsaking Him, and ask Him to forgive us. Then there must be a wholesale turning away from sinful wicked behavior.

The decision is this: Do you believe that God is? Do you believe that He rewards all those who believe He is and who place their trust in Him by faith in the death and resurrection of Jesus Christ for eternal life through the forgiveness of your sins? Do you then by faith live a life that seeks to honor Him daily?

The history of the world is really His story of the incarnation, Jesus Christ, God become flesh, who dwelt among men speaking to them of the Kingdom of God and salvation freely offered to all mankind.

Today I encourage you to place your faith in Jesus Christ, turn from your sin, and become a disciple. Live your life from this day forward by the power of God and for His glory and honor.

If you would like to know more about how to place your faith in Jesus Christ and become a child of God you may email me – pastormike@cclohio.org

God bless you today as you seek Him.

Chapter Nineteen

"Encouragement Through a Realistic Appraisal of Our Times"

Perseverance is an admirable quality but without faithfulness to God it is really meaningless. People persevere in the wrong things all the time. Faithfulness sets you apart.

As I consider the times in which we live, I see faithfulness as increasingly rare. I see compromise everywhere. I see Christians supporting:

- Same sex unions because all that really matters is love, right?
- LGBT propaganda; marching in what I call "shame" parades because there is certainly nothing to be proud of related to what men to do each other or women to women in the name of their definition of love.

- The murder of pre-born human beings.
- The casting aside of the rule of law for the rule of the mob; violence in our streets.

America is in the fast lane on a runaway train that is headed for a crash. The politicians in Washington DC have capitulated to the dark forces of evil that have in these days revealed themselves.

Those that hate America, hate the fact that Americans are free, and more importantly hate God, are now center stage, encouraging violence against conservatives AND Christians, the latter being the real target.

There is a reason why Christians are being targeted for lawsuits by radicalized ideologically driven useful idiots. There is a reason why mobs of angry people oppose political candidates who express Christian faith. The reason is America has birthed God-haters.

We allowed God-haters to incubate in the 1960-70's when they removed prayer and Bible reading from public schools. We allowed them to tell us that sodomy was not an abomination before God, but that it is merely a sexual preference.

We allowed God-haters to grow in power and strength through demonic blood offerings of abortion. Today, the enemies of God are loud and proud, as the saying goes.

What has this silence by the church resulted in today? We read almost daily now about another school bringing in drag queens to entertain our pre-school and young children. We read of schools telling parents to shut up and mind their own business when they teach our children that transgenderism is normal, that our children should explore their sexuality and go in whatever direction they "feel" is right for them.

I read the headlines and the insanity that has gripped America has one explanation: it is demonic. Listen to me folks; we are not experiencing a cultural difference of opinion. We are in the throes of a full-fledged demonic attack aimed at destroying this nation and some Christians are too ignorant to see it.

We have people advocating for socialism within the church! The political theory of Marxism is the foundation of socialism and it is satanic to its very core. Yet, ignorant Christians are extolling its biblical virtues of fairness. This is a special kind of spiritual blindness.

BUT, in this climate, in this darkness, the glorious light of God shines brightest for those willing to be used of God to be a beacon of truth and righteousness.

In this present darkness the true body of Jesus Christ must arise. I am reminded of the story of Esther. Do you recall the events surrounding God's working through His people in the events given to us in the book of Esther? Let me summarize.

- King Ahasuerus reigned over a kingdom that stretched from the present day Middle East all the way to India.
- Queen Vashti was summoned, refused, and deposed.
- Esther became Queen;
- Mordecai, Esther's uncle who raised her as his daughter, discovered a plot to assassinate King Ahasuerus and saved the Kings life.
- King Ahasuerus promoted Haman the Agagite, likely an Amalekite descended from Esau, sworn enemies of the Jews, to a place of prominence in the kingdom.
- Mordechai refused to bow or honor Haman.
- Haman decides to trick King Ahasuerus into signing a proclamation to allow for the extermination of the Jews throughout his kingdom.

That brings us to chapter 4 of Esther. Please read verses 13-14. I say this to true believers today: you stand as faithful servants of the Most High God for such a time as this.

An overwhelming number of Christians have retreated from the battlefield. Indeed many have sided with the enemy thinking they will survive the coming destruction.

But, make no mistake, the demonic forces that have been unleashed upon America have an objective: it is you, the church, and ultimately in their demonic insanity, our Father and our Lord Jesus Christ.

Let me show you their plan. Turn with me to Psalm 2. Here we find the clearest explanation for what we see happening in America and across the earth today.

What do we find in this Psalm? We see governments and political leaders in an uproar. We see them secretly planning their coup, making their plans to attack and conquer (v. 1-2). Against who are their plans aimed? Their goal is to overthrow Yahweh, the God of the Bible AND His "Anointed." Who is that? It is the Lord Jesus Christ (v. 12). The primary focus of their plan is to destroy the foundations of Christianity which is the Bible and the teachings it contains. In other words, the governments, politicians, and heathen rage against God's standards, against His objective truth, against what He declares to be right and wrong. That is verse 3. The God-haters desire to "tear their (Yahweh and Jesus Christ) fetters apart and cast away their cords." The God-haters do not want to be bound by God's commands and so they devise their plans to overthrow Him throughout the world. They are driven by a controlled lust to be free of God's influence.

Who is in control of the kings of the earth? Who is in control of the governments of the world? Who is in control of all those who believe their wealth, their power, their influence means that they have the right to make decisions for the entire world?

Answer: Satan and those to whom he delegates that authority. We call them demons.

Matthew 4:8-10 says:

> *Again, the devil took Him to a very high mountain and showed Him all the kingdoms of the world and their glory; and he said to Him, "All these things I will give You, if You fall down and worship me." Then Jesus said to him, "Go, Satan! For it is written, 'YOU SHALL WORSHIP THE LORD YOUR GOD, AND SERVE HIM ONLY.'"*

2 Corinthians 4:1-4 says this:

> *Therefore, since we have this ministry, as we received mercy, we do not lose heart, but we have renounced the things hidden because of shame, not walking in craftiness or adulterating the word of God, but by the manifestation of truth commending ourselves to every man's conscience in the sight of God. And even if our gospel is veiled, it is veiled to those who are perishing, in whose case the god of this world has blinded the minds of the unbelieving so that they might not see the light of the gospel of the glory of Christ, who is the image of God.*

Friends, we are told plainly in Ephesians 6 that we are at war with Satan and his followers. Turn with me to that passage. Look specifically at verse 12.

What I have come to understand after 35 years of walking with Christ is that too many Christians are ignorant of what this verse and this passage is telling us. They say, "People aren't the enemy. Satan is the enemy. It says right here that we don't fight against flesh and blood."

That is a misreading of the text, a misunderstanding of the testimony of Scripture, and is evidence of the mass ignorance pervasive among believers today.

Satan and those he controls is our enemy because they are the enemy of God.

Acts 2:32-35 is Peter's Pentecost sermon in which the apostle said:

> *This Jesus God raised up again, to which we are all witnesses. Therefore having been exalted to the right hand of God, and having received from the Father the promise of the Holy Spirit, He has poured forth this which you both see and hear. For it was not David who ascended into heaven, but he himself says:*
>
> *'THE LORD SAID TO MY LORD,*
> *"SIT AT MY RIGHT HAND,*
> *UNTIL I MAKE YOUR ENEMIES A FOOTSTOOL FOR YOUR FEET."'*

The apostle Paul says in Romans 5:10:

> *For if while we were enemies we were reconciled to God through the death of His Son, much more, having been reconciled, we shall be saved by His life.*

James 4:4:

> *You adulteresses, do you not know that friendship with the world is hostility toward God? Therefore whoever wishes to be a friend of the world makes himself an enemy of God.*

So what is a demon? Look again Ephesians 6:12. We see rulers (Greek *archon*), powers (Greek *exousiazo*), world forces of darkness (Greek *kosmokrator*), and spiritual forces of wickedness (Greek *pneumatikos*) and their home is the supernatural realm. That's what "heavenly places" means.

Demons are entities without bodies. They are in my opinion the disembodied spirits of the Nephilim. BUT they will always look for a body. We can look to the public ministry of Jesus to see this fact.

How many demons did Jesus cast out of people in His three years of ministry? Probably in the tens of thousands. Do you recall the demon possessed man of the Gadarenes? He was filled with a legion of demons which is the equivalent of six thousand. Do you remember their request when Jesus commanded them to leave the man? They asked to enter the pigs. Demons always look for a body to possess.

Friends, we are seeing the full disclosure today, the manifestation of the spiritual warfare that has gone on since the creation. We are witnessing the war between the seed of the woman and the seed of the serpent that God declared would characterize mankind's existence until He sent His redeemer, the Lord Jesus Christ to crush the head of Satan.

Genesis 3:14-15 says:

The LORD God said to the serpent,

> *"Because you have done this,*
> *Cursed are you more than all cattle,*
> *And more than every beast of the field;*
> *On your belly you will go,*
> *And dust you will eat*
> *All the days of your life;*
> *And I will put enmity*
> *Between you and the woman,*
> *And between your seed and her seed;*
> *He shall bruise you on the head,*
> *And you shall bruise him on the heel."*

This is why we are instructed in Ephesians 6:10 to "be strong in the Lord and in the strength of His might." I encourage you to also take note of 6:10-11, 13, and 18. Now, how do we attain these things? How do we persevere in the face of such evil in our day? Let me show you a picture of how we become strong in the Lord, how we prepare ourselves to successfully persevere. Turn with me in your Bible to 2 Kings 2.

In 2 Kings 2 we see the narrative concerning the transition of the prophetic office from Elijah to Elisha. Elisha earnestly desired to continue God's powerful work that He had demonstrated through Elijah.

In fact Elisha desired even more of God's holy fire. Note 2 Kings 2:9. A double portion? Amen! I want a double portion of God's anointing resting upon me, don't you? So Elisha boldly asked for a double portion of power from God.

Notice Elijah's response in verse 10. In other words if you go with me till the end, if you persevere with me God will honor you. So here is my question for you today friends: what does it take to persevere? Let's find out.

Let's start at 2 Kings 2:1. The journey of perseverance starts at Gilgal. Gilgal is the place of preparation. Gilgal means "the rolling away" or "the putting off."

When Joshua assumed leadership of the Hebrew people, they arrive at a place on the opposite side of the Jordan before entering the Promised Land. There God told them to circumcise the men.

Remember this generation grew up during the wilderness wandering after all the men over twenty years old perished for refusing to enter the Promised Land the first time. God essentially told them that before you can enter into the fullness of the land of promise which I have given to you, before you can have victory over the enemy that you will have to defeat, there must first come a putting off of the flesh, a rolling away of the flesh.

And so the Hebrew people named the place Gilgal – the place of putting away the flesh. This was their preparation. Before we can experience God's blessings, before He will use us in this great spiritual war we are called to, there must be a putting off of the flesh. You must empty yourself before you can be filled.

Before God can use you effectively there must be a house cleaning. We must get rid of the junk (flesh) in our lives. The sin, the iniquity, anything that keeps us from complete surrender to God must be put off and forsaken.

Then in verse 2 we read that Elijah and Elisha traveled to Bethel. After the place of preparation comes Bethel. Do you recall the story? Jacob and Esau were brothers. God told their mother that the older (Esau) would serve the younger (Jacob). Conflict ensued that marked their entire lives. Jacob was coerced into deceiving his father Isaac for his older brother Esau's blessing.

When Esau found out he vowed to kill Jacob so Jacob had to flee. During his flight from Esau, Jacob stopped to sleep at a place named Luz and there received a vision/dream from God where he saw angels ascending and descending on a staircase.

Jacob proclaimed "Surely God is in this place and I did not know it." He named the place Bethel which means "the house of God." So after preparation (Gilgal) comes realization (Bethel) that God is with me and for me. What a powerful truth this is. When God calls you to prepare yourself, and you obey that calling, He will give with that an assurance of His presence with you.

Once we do away with hindrances to complete surrender to God we must realize that God's presence is with us wherever we go. He will bless us with His good gifts to do all He calls us to do. Where God guides God provides.

Jesus said "if you being evil know how to give good gifts to your children how much more does the heavenly Father give good gifts and the Holy Spirit to them that ask?"[14] God does not call us to battle in this spiritual war without equipping us from His divine armory.[15]

This is God's plan: to call you to preparation, to give you assurance of His presence through the gifts of His Spirit

---

[14] Matthew 7:11. Unless otherwise state, all Scripture references are from the New American Standard Bible, Lockman Foundation, 1978.
[15] Ephesians 6:11-18.

and His divine armor. That is the Apostle Paul's point in Ephesians 2:10: "For we are His workmanship, created in Christ Jesus for good works, which God prepared beforehand so that we would walk in them."

Now, after preparation (getting rid of the flesh that hinders our walk), you will come to realize that God is with you and for you and will provide all you need (His good gifts including His armor). After these steps comes the test of readiness. Issuing weapons to soldiers without providing training in their use is a dangerous strategy.

Let's look at 2 Kings 2:3-4 to see the next step in God's plan to equip us to persevere. In these verses we see the city of Jericho. It is the place of confrontation. Do you recall the history? After the Hebrews left Gilgal, the place of preparation, they came to Jericho.

God gave them specific instructions about His battle plan. They were not to attack but instead they were to march around the city for seven days. On the seventh day they shouted and the walls came down. What is the picture? This pictures the power of God through His Holy Spirit in the lives of His people. The power of God exercised through obedient Christians cannot be defeated. The purposes of God will be accomplished through obedience to His commands regardless of the circumstances we might face.

God gives us the Holy Spirit to fight, to engage the enemy. Jesus tells us the same thing in Acts 1:8 – you will receive power when the Holy Spirit comes upon you, and you will be His witnesses everywhere and in every context. The power of the Holy Spirit is given to all prepared believers who know in whom they have trusted so that we can run TO the battle not away from the battle.

Then in verses 5-6 we see the Jordan. On the other side was the land of promise. It was within view now. What does the Jordan picture for us? The Jordan pictures the place of expectation.

Remember the story: the Hebrew people were ready to enter into the land after decades of wandering the desert. God told Joshua to have the priests come forward with the Ark of the Covenant and merely stand on the edge of the river with the feet in the water.

Why? Because simple obedience leads to God's glory. What happened when the priests did as they were instructed? God parted the Jordan and the people entered into the Promised Land.

The picture is this friends: Step out in faith with full assurance and expectation that God will provide, bless, and bring His plans for you to fruition. So let me summarize what we have learned.

Perseverance is built upon:

- Preparation (Gilgal – getting rid of the flesh)
- Realization (Bethel – realizing that God is with us and for us)
- Confrontation (Jericho – we confront evil in the power of the Holy Spirit)
- Expectation (Jordan – God will be glorified in us and through our obedience)

Remember the words of Moses to the Israelites as they were poised to enter into God's Promised Land. This spiritual principle holds true for us as well.

> *Be strong and courageous, do not be afraid or tremble at them, for the LORD your God is the one who goes with you. He will not fail you or forsake you.*[16]

I remind you of Peter's words of encouragement:

> *But you are A CHOSEN RACE, A royal PRIESTHOOD, A HOLY NATION, A PEOPLE FOR God's OWN POSSESSION, so that you may proclaim the excellencies of Him who has called you out of darkness into His marvelous light;*[17]

---

[16] Deuteronomy 31:6.

[17] 1 Peter 2:9

My prayer for you is that as long as the Lord tarries you will continue to press on for the upward call in Christ Jesus. Do not fear the demoniacs that have seized our government, our politicians, and our culture, including the leftist progressive apostates who believe they represent Christ. Rebels represent their father Satan[18] not the Lord Jesus Christ. Be bold and courageous and take the fight to the enemy of God with confidence.

---

[18] John 8:44.

Chapter Twenty

The "NEW" Atheism: Another Skirmish With a Twist

The year was A.D. 17 and the Roman Empire was once again flexing its muscle along the vast European wilderness. A young Roman general by the name of Germanicus was swiftly becoming a favorite son of the Romans due to his bloodline and reports of his military victories in Germania. A great-nephew to Augustus, he had the inside track to the throne and imperial power. A last minute appeal by the wife of Augustus secured the throne for her son Tiberius. As a concession to naming Tiberius heir to the throne, Germanicus was formally adopted as a son by Tiberius and declared successor to him.

Tiberius would have been content to allow Germanicus to remain in the wilderness fighting the barbarians if not for the growing popularity of his general among the Roman citizens. Each new report of victory for the legions under his command brought about public discussion of his worthiness to rule Rome. In order to stop Germanicus' popularity from eclipsing his own, Tiberius sent word to Germanicus to return to Rome at once to receive a hero's welcome and the honor of a "triumph," the victor's parade reserved exclusively for Rome's military heroes who demonstrated exceptional valor on the battlefield and who achieved devastating defeats of Rome's enemies.

Not much has changed in relation to war heroes over the last two millennia. Successful warriors are still rewarded and admired. The battlefield that this paper will describe is not one of actual physical combat but instead is the battlefield of the mind. Ideas have become conquering heroes to many and the so-called new atheism is certainly engaged in a battle for the minds of the Western world. Some have accepted atheism as having vanquished its most formidable foe – Christian theism. This paper will make clear that assumption is false.

WHAT'S "NEW" ABOUT ATHEISM?

As recently as 2005 atheism was declared a dying philosophical belief system.[19] Reasons for this belief abound and include the fact that atheism at its core is

---

[19]Alister E. McGrath and Neil Brennan, "The Twilight of Atheism," *Christianity Today.* 49 (March 2005):36-40.

derivative. That is to say that the atheistic belief system is viable so long as it has a host – religion in general and increasingly Christianity in particular - to draw its sustenance from and perform its parasitic work upon. Removed from its host and forced to stand on its own merits atheism has little to say by way of articulating a belief system that is livable. Additionally, atheism appears to be unaware of or unconcerned that its dependence on modernity for its philosophical foundation leaves it vulnerable and easily discarded as a failed relic in a postmodern culture.

The question "what is new about atheism" deserves investigation and the formulation of a robust answer. Some attribute the new atheist's popularity to the backlash against a supposed evangelical White House under President Bush and the sometimes foolish, arrogant, and hypocritical statements and behaviors of American evangelicals.[20] Popular culture, although never an accurate barometer of actual movements given the fickleness and ease of manipulation, would suggest that atheism is not dead after all. The widespread acceptance of new forms of spiritual expression hiding atheistic roots including Wicca and Yoga, seem to suggest a still vibrant undertow of religious conviction albeit subjective and God denying. It seems appropriate to borrow a phrase from sports commentator Lee Corso, who would say, "Not so fast my

[20]David Aikman, "Puncturing Atheism: Fourfold God Squad Brilliantly Takes on Dawkins, Hitchens, & Co." *Christianity Today*. 51 (October 2007):110.

friend" in response to the assertion that atheism has lost its impact on American culture.

ATHEISM IS BEING REPACKAGED

Fox Television Network has a blockbuster hit in their evening programming lineup. Since 2004 the show *House* has gained popularity such that today it boasts of consistent Top 10 ratings among all shows and is the top rated Fox drama show.[21] Some might say this is no big deal. Television has lots of shows that claim to be "top rated." *House* is different from other shows and is a big deal to cultural observers because it features a lead actor who portrays an atheist medical doctor. Consider the following conversations from several shows between actor Hugh Laurie who plays Dr. House and various characters that portray believers in other faith systems:

Sister Eucharist: I need to talk with you, Dr. House. Sister Augustine believes in things that aren't real.

House: I thought that was a job requirement for you people.

Then there's this exchange with the orthodox Jewish husband of a sick woman.

House: You live according to God's six hundred commandments, right?

---

[21]Neilson Ratings available at http://tvlistings.zap2it.com/ratings/weekly.html Accessed March 30, 2009.

Husband: [folding his arms] Six hundred thirteen.

House: You understand them all?

Husband: Takes a lifetime of learning...

House: But you follow the ones you don't understand because the ones you do understand make sense, and you believe the guy who created them knows what he's doing.

Husband: Of course.

House: So you will trust my diagnosis and you'll let me treat her, because in this temple, [scarify] I am Dr. Yahweh.

Husband [with look of disbelief]: I want a new doctor.

As a Champion of Atheism, Gregory House has won the show some shout-outs from the secular side, happy to embrace any plausible primetime soul mate. A House video clip can be found on the website of Richard Dawkins, Oxford professor and author of the bestselling *The God Delusion*.

In it, the doctor tells a fellow physician that his patient's newly found religious faith is only a symptom of disease.

Physician: We can't just inject her with " 10cc of atheism and send her home.

House: Religion is a symptom of irrational belief based on groundless hope.[22]

---

[22]Christine McCarthy McMorris, "Playing Godless," *Religion in the News.* 11

This new softer gentler atheism is also appearing on the big screen. December 2007 witnessed the release of the critically acclaimed *The Golden Compass* in movie theaters across America. Billed as a delightful and adventurous children's story, *The Golden Compass* is the first book in a trilogy from author Philip Pullman entitled *His Dark Materials*. This trilogy presents Pullman's belief that the idea of God is nonsense and that only mankind can save itself. Although presenting a seemingly innocuous atheism Pullman takes pains to insure his point is made as evidenced by the following line in the movie spoken by a former nun to two children explaining why she no longer believed in God and left the Christian faith behind: (Christianity is) "a very powerful and convincing mistake, that's all."[23] Pullman includes in his movie such things as a magic knife named *Aesahaettr* which means god-destroyer, a reenactment of the Fall of mankind in the Garden of Eden, but with the effect of saving the universe not subjecting it to judgment, and perhaps most telling of all, a presentation of the biblical God not as Creator but as imposter, cheat, and liar who deceives mankind into believing that He is a supreme being.

Observers given to a more investigative nature will notice Pullman's penchant for Platonism and Gnostic mythology especially as it relates to God as an Old Testament evil.

(Spring 2008):20-21.

[23]Peter T. Chattaway, "The Chronicles of Atheism," *Christianity Today*. 51 (December 2007):36-39.

His use of the term *daemon* for the spirit guides of children is an unmistakable reference to the demiurge of the Gnostics.

The Golden Compass is nothing more than Pullman's atheistic belief system presented as a children's tale.

These examples show that atheism is making inroads into American culture and thought life even as the horse of Troy was accepted without discernment. Atheism appears to be merely another life choice to many Americans. Some have opined that atheism is experiencing a rise in popularity not seen since the days of Nietzsche.[24] The triumvirate of Richard Dawkins, Christopher Hitchins, and Samuel Harris seem to have seized this opportunity and have written recent diatribes against Christianity. Hitchens says in his book *God Is Not Great: How Religion Poisons Everything* that, "Many of the teachings of Christianity are, as well as being incredible and mythical, immoral."[25]

Dawkins gives advice to Christians everywhere who speak out against atheism, encouraging them to "just shut up."[26] In an interview in 2004 Dawkins could not find a single thing of redeeming worth within religion. When pressed to cite even one minor thing that religion has done for the good Dawkins responded, "No, I really can't think of

---

[24]Stan Guthrie, "Answering the Atheists," *Christianity Today* (November 2007), 74.

[25]Ibid., 74.

[26]Ibid., 74.

anything."[27]   Other new atheists have been equally vocal recently.   Daniel Dennett for example hopes for a day when science will provide enough evidence to "break the spell" of religion.[28]

The media has not been as accepting as would be expected. This very same press that Christians and conservatives alike consider beyond rehabilitation has taken the new atheists to task through surprisingly tepid, critical reviews.   Consider for instance the following responses by the media to the writings of these three authors:

> (The) *Washington Post's* religion writer David Segal wrote on October 26, 2006, that Harris's writings are "straight out of the stun grenade school of public rhetoric."; So negative are the New Atheists that their impact will be merely to "elevate the rancor in our public discussion," claimed *New York Sun* columnist John McWhorter on May 24, 2007; In addition, journalists found fault with the New Atheists' knowledge of theology and religion, the main subject matter of their books. Dawkins failed to "appreciate just how hard philosophical questions about religion can be," freelancer Jim Holt wrote in the *New York Times* October 22, 2006, while Dennett missed "the actual substance of religious

---

[27]Available at www.belief.net Cited in Stephen M. Barr, "The Devil's Chaplain Confounded," *First Things* (August-September 2004), 29.

[28]Daniel Dennett, *Breaking the Spell: Religion as a Natural Phenomenon* (New York, NY: Viking, 2006), 39. Cited in Carlos R. Bovell, "If Scientists Can Naturalize God, Should Philosophers Re-Supernaturalize Him?" *Theology Today* vol. 64 (2007): 340-348.

experience," according to the *New York Sun's* Adam Kirsch, on February 8, 2006. As for Harris, sniffed Steinfels of the *Times* on March 3, 2007, he failed to "engage religious thought in any serious way." The *Miami Herald's* Alter thus described Dawkins as "the world's foremost evangelical atheist," who denounced the evils of religion "in tones that resemble the giddy zeal of a tent revivalist." In a January 7 (2007) article in the *Chicago Sun-Times*, Huffington Post blogger R. J. Eskow called - Dennett and Dawkins "fundamentalist atheists" who "use scientific thought in much the same way religious fundamentalists use sacred text—as the source for unquestionable and rigid truths that can't be challenged."[29]

THE CURRENT PHILOSOPHICAL CLIMATE

In his *Critique of Pure Reason* Immanuel Kant established what has been termed the "Enlightenment Fallacy." Kant demonstrated that mankind can never acquire enough knowledge to comprehend completely the whole of reality. Reason is simply not capable of comprehending and articulating the entirety of what can and might be known. Instead of answering questions satisfactorily Kant

---

[29]Bernard Lightman, "Beating Up On the New Atheists," *Religion in the News*. 10 (Sum-Fall 2007):2-4.

suggested that human reason raises questions that it is incapable of answering. Kant pointed to the idea of reality and mankind's existence within it and asked how we acquire knowledge of truth. This is one reason why the new atheists reject Kantian thought associated with this subject. Kant insisted that there was more to know than what our five senses alone could tell us. The idea that what we experience does not contain the whole of knowledge is antithetical to the atheist. Thus atheism rejects any concept of metaphysics, the very thing that Kantian thought placed beyond the realm of human reason to adequately grasp and articulate. This response from the new atheism is not unexpected. If there is something we cannot see, hear, smell, touch, or feel, and which is beyond our ability to study empirically then science is shown to be a fraud for claiming that it is the final authority in determining what can be known. Atheists understand that scientific naturalism is a system of absolute values just like Christian theism. Clearly, atheists prefer scientific naturalism and reject Christian theism and therefore the question of God. The possibility that God exists is nonsensical within their belief system.

Enlightenment Modernism characterized by its dependence on and faith in scientific naturalism and intellectual rationalism has been exposed much like the emperor in Andersen's fabled children's story. Postmodernism, in replacing modernism has taken a scorched earth approach to both intellectual and practical cultural engagement. Any and every field of inquiry is fair game to the deconstructionist's guillotine. While Christianity has certainly not escaped postmodernism's scathing critiques, it has faired far better than its secular counterparts. Christianity has always been forthright in its confession that faith operates by supposition and therefore Christian theism stares down postmodernism at this point. Christians believe certain things based on certain other things that are taken for granted. Of primary importance is the belief that God exists. Science on the other hand had, until postmodernism captured the academic fortresses, believed it was a system of empirically observable truths not based on presupposition.

Marxist-Atheist philosopher Richard Lewontin for example believes that the reason Americans reject the scientific explanation of the origin of life as embodied in Darwinian evolutionary theory is not due to ignorance of the facts but instead is located in "starting point" or worldview bias: "The primary problem is not to provide the public with the knowledge of how far it is to the nearest star and what genes are made of . . . rather, the problem is to get them to reject irrational and supernatural explanations of the world, the demons that exist only in their imaginations, and to accept a social and intellectual apparatus, Science, as the only begetter of truth."[30] Apparently lost on Lewontin is the fact that his own certitude related to scientific naturalism is itself a belief system based on presupposition and as such his assertions to the contrary make him appear

---

[30]Phillip E. Johnson, "The Unraveling of Scientific Naturalism," *First Things* (November 1997): 22-25.

naïve, deceived or both. Likewise, Daniel Dennett betrays the same presupposition in his recent book entitled, *Breaking the Spell: Religion as a Natural Phenomenon,* aimed at encouraging a study of human religion from an evolutionary standpoint. His goal is simply to "propose further scientific investigations of religion to be undertaken by competent researchers, and to suggest what forms of public policy we might wish, as a society, to adopt in regard to religion, once we have begun to acquire a proper understanding of its nature."[31]   Postmodernism has brought an end to these unchallenged axioms of scientific naturalists and atheists alike.   The skirmish has been engaged by postmodern philosophy and atheism is a victim in the assault.

This turn of events is fortunate for Christianity. Previously most scientists were unwilling to discuss ideas, theories, or research that suggested alternatives to existing scientific dogma involving a beginning of the universe.   By challenging scientific naturalism postmodernism has opened the door for Christian scientists to discuss evidence of energy fields, the movements of galaxies, subatomic particles, and quantum physics within the context of a starting point for the universe.

One would think that in such a climate the new atheists would tread lightly or in the least demonstrate a degree of humility. Such is not the case. Instead of answering the

---

[31]David B. Hart, "Daniel Dennett Hunts the Snark," *First Things,* (January 2007): 30-38.

challenge of postmodernism, atheists have retreated more deeply into the abyss of scientism. Perhaps this is so because Dawkins, Hitchins, Harris, and their peers cannot answer the charges of postmodernism. One is left to believe that the unwillingness of the new atheists to face the rigor of debate is in principle a declaration that they cannot with any sustainable intellectual power provide a framework of solutions that demonstrate atheism's superiority. Perhaps the new atheists believe that because their pronouncements are made with sincerity and frequency they are somehow transformed into unquestionable fact.

Haught provides a strong argument that the new atheists are nothing more than weak-kneed, self-deluded, presuppositional idealists as compared to classical atheists such as Marx, Freud, Camus, and Sartre. He suggests that "scientism is . . . the self-subverting creed that provides the spongy cognitive foundation of the entire project we are dignifying with the label "new atheism."[32] When atheists proclaim that science alone is the final arbiter of truth, that science alone is the only methodology of understanding, they are in fact making a declaration of faith. In so doing they have offered a "do as I say and not as I do" approach because while telling people to take nothing on faith but always defer to empirical evidence, i.e. scientific methods, they have themselves succumbed to accepting the scientific method by faith. Christopher Hitchens is oblivious to his

---

[32]John F. Haught, "Amateur Atheists," *Christian Century* (February 2008): 22-28.

predicament and says, "If one must have faith in order to believe something, then the likelihood of that something having any truth or value is considerably diminished."[33] Of course this statement is self-refuting because there is no empirical evidence to prove this statement is true. Hitchens thus becomes victim to the very thing he roundly criticizes in Christian theists, namely presupposition. A more obvious atheistic presuppositional bias is provided by Lewontin who says, "We take the side of science in spite of the patent absurdity of some of its constructs, in spite of its failure to fulfill many of its extravagant promises of health and life, in spite of the tolerance of the scientific community for unsubstantiated just-so stories, because we have a prior commitment – a commitment to materialism . . . Moreover, that materialism is absolute, for we cannot allow a Divine Foot in the door."[34]

Lewontin's admission is clearly the crux of the matter for the new atheists. At issue is not that the new atheists won't admit to the presence of adequate evidence and clear logical reasons for believing that God exists. The primary issue for them is that they do not want to believe that God exists. For the atheist the resultant implications of allowing the "Divine Foot" through the door are unsavory to say the least. What Lewontin as well as his peers refuse to understand is that evolutionary theory encroaches on metaphysical matters of importance to Christians and thus

[33]Ibid., 22.
[34]Dinesh D'Souza, "What's So Great About Christianity" (Washington D.C.: Regnery Publishing, 2007), 161.

has opened wide the door for God to in the least enter the discussion. Some examples from evolutionary theory prove this point. Evolutionary theory offers a story of origins and therefore the concepts of creation are open to debate by the Christian theist; Evolution suggests an origin story for human life and thus it touches on the biblical teaching of original sin; Evolution also speaks of species and uniqueness and therefore touches on the biblical teaching of the image of God in man.[35]

Steven Weinberg, National Medal of Science award winner and Noble laureate in physics presented a clear picture of what is at stake. The issue for Weinberg and other atheist scientists is found in their quest for freedom from religion. Consider these comments presented in an address to the American Association for the Advancement of Science in 1999: "One of the great achievements of science has been, if not to make it impossible for intelligent people to be religious, then at least to make it possible for them to not be religious. We should not retreat from this accomplishment . . . With or without religion, good people can behave well and bad people can do evil; but for good people to do evil – that takes religion."[36] It is notable that Lewontin does not offer any examples to bolster this claim.

The unstated assumption by the new atheists is that life

---

[35]Gregory R. Peterson, "Whose evolution? Which theology?" *Zygon.* 35 (June 2000): 221-232.

[36]Philip Hefner, "Modern and Postmodern Forms of Unbelief," *The Christian Century* (January 2000), 89.

without God would continue just as it currently does. Dawkins, Hitchens, and Harris believe that life as we know it with all the modern conveniences of law, order, justice, altruism, and civility would simply continue unfettered. This viewpoint is contradicted by the classical atheists. Sartre understood rightly that atheism accepted and lived out would be a cruel teacher. He surmised that the vast majority of mankind could never come to grips with atheism because they would be too weak to accept the consequences of the death of God. Nietzsche experienced the consequences of a world without God – a rabid nihilism well beyond skepticism that left him broken and hedonistic. Perhaps the new atheists have deliberated on the truths of Sartre, Nietzsche, and Camus and having seen the devastation that their belief system brings have chosen atheism "light."

C.S. Lewis in "Men without Chests" provides a scathing critique of the new atheist's position stated above. Lewis asserted that for people to be moral in the most basic sense, the head must rule the stomach. What Lewis meant was that reason must rule emotion. This is only accomplished when the head has been informed by the will – the chest in his essay. The problem in Lewis's day is the same we experience today, namely that modern man and his dependence on rationalism has equated morality with knowledge but not action. Consequently the will is subjected to the passions and morality has become a bankrupt and vacuous term. Lewis famously summed up the quagmire by saying, "We make men without chests and expect of them virtue and enterprise. We laugh at honor and are shocked to find traitors in our midst. We castrate and bid the geldings be fruitful."[37] What the new atheists denounce is the very thing that can save mankind – the possibility of the transformation of the human heart, Lewis's "chest," by the God who designed us.

SCIENCE CANNOT ANSWER THE GOD QUESTION

Is a system that is purposely designed to deny the existence of God the best platform from which to address the question of God? Is it even capable of answering metaphysical questions? Richard Dawkins believes that science can answer the question of God's existence because science is the depository of all relevant evidence. When Dawkins speaks of relevant evidence he is referring to that evidence derived from empirical experimentation. In the least Dawkins and the other new atheists referred to in this paper are being disingenuous when they talk of answering the God question from within a system that does not allow for His existence. Consistency is not a feature of the new atheism apparently.

Science answers questions within the natural realm. God exists beyond the natural realm and is not subjected to the so-called observable laws of nature. Thus it bears repeating that a belief system, be it atheism or scientific naturalism

---

[37]C.S. Lewis, *The Abolition of Man* (New York, NY: Macmillan, 1947), 35.

that denies the possibility of God, indeed excludes any input from a metaphysical viewpoint is ill-suited to attempt to answer the metaphysical questions concerning God. Indeed the new atheist's commentary on God is itself nonsensical by their own standard.

The New Atheists spend huge amounts of time and resources discussing issues that cannot be answered within their faith system. Reason has its limits despite Hume's emphasis on empirical verifiability and the subsequent logical positivism that developed as a result. Thus it requires asking the question of why the new atheists are so vehemently opposed to Christian theism. What is at stake for them?

CHRISTIAN THEISM ANSWERS WHAT ATHEISM CANNOT

The current debate between atheism and Christian theism is not deadlocked as some suppose. There is not an insurmountable mountain of evidence that bolsters the atheist's claim to have defeated Christianity. To the contrary, the evidence demonstrates movement in the ongoing academic debate. As Johnson points out, "both sides are near agreement on a redefinition of the conflict. Biblical literalism is not the issue. The issue is whether materialism and rationality is the same thing. Darwinism is based on an a priori commitment to materialism, not on a philosophically neutral assessment of the evidence. Separate the philosophy from the science, and the proud tower collapses."[38]

Many others see the same thing emerging in the broader debates between scientific naturalists and Christian theists. The rhetoric of the new atheists "betrays panic, another sign of weakness. Atheism knows that it is losing both arguments and the global tide. Stories of the global vibrancy of religion are everywhere trumping the grand narrative of evolutionary progress. And the best philosophers are still taking the God-hypothesis seriously."[39]

Daniel Maguire suggests that atheists cannot escape God-talk because it is wired into their subconciousness as a condition of their humanity.[40] Indeed the *imago dei* is not easily suppressed and man is less able to escape the intellectual struggle entered into when denying God. To do so would require atheists to invent new moral foundations for ethics, morals, modern bills of rights, as well as due-process theories of justice. Dawkins believes this can be done. He states that "at the same time I support Darwinism as a scientist, I am a passionate anti-Darwinian when it comes to politics and how we should conduct our human affairs."[41] What Dawkins means by that somewhat

---

[38]Johnson, 25.

[39]"The New Intolerance: Fear-mongering Among Elite Atheists Is Not a Pretty Sight," *Christianity Today*. 51 (February 2007):24-25.

[40]Daniel C. Maguire, "Atheists for Jesus: The Moral Core of Religious Experience," *Christian Century*. 110 (December 1993):1228-1230.

[41]Stephen M. Barr, "The Devil's Chaplain Confounded," *First Things* (August-September 2004): 25-30.

shocking statement is revealed in his book *The Selfish Gene,* in which he says "We, alone on earth, can rebel against the tyranny of the selfish replicator" . . . because mankind has been accidently endowed with intelligence by a mindless nature and this "blessed gift of understanding" is for Dawkins responsible for human morality.[42]

Against the intellectual dead-end and schizophrenia of the new atheism Christianity offers hope rooted in objective truth. The Christian theistic worldview offers a satisfying and consistent understanding of the universe because it is presented within a context of a God who loves it and created it with special purpose. Randomness and chance evaporate into a sea of meaning. The Christian theistic view speaks of time and space as having meaning. Time is viewed as a linear characteristic of the universe, meaning that not only was there a beginning to all that currently is but that time is also moving toward a climax or ending. The Christian worldview makes sense of the physical evidence even now being discovered and validated by scientists who are anything but Christian.

The Christian worldview also speaks of the rationality of the creation. Because God is a rational being His creation has rational characteristics. The Bible says that God created mankind in His image. This means that people have inherent worth and value in God's eyes in spite of the sin that dominates so many. This is why Christianity upholds the sanctity of life and takes strong stands against

---

[42]Ibid., 26.

policies and practices that seek to wantonly destroy human life.

The new atheism has not succeeded in escaping the transcendent nature of values. Christian theists have told them they will not be able to. Each will have to find out on their own. Their forerunners Nietzsche, Sartre, and Camus stepped back from the abyss of radical atheism once the fullness of the evil it would unleash upon mankind was realized in their own souls. They understood albeit late in life, that mankind is a moral creature because there is a moral God. They stopped short of confessing this publically and clearly but their prescriptions for life without God betrayed what they knew to be true intellectually.

Nietzsche for example wrote that man without God should live lives of creativity and purpose, surely transcendent values; Sartre's existentialism morphed into humanism where he began to speak of basic human rights, a grudgingly and verbally unacknowledged salute toward transcendence; and even Camus' literary career betrayed his professed atheism as his preoccupation with moral guilt in *The Fall* attests.

CONCLUSION

Tiberius's honoring of Germanicus with a victory parade was a charade from start to finish. By calling Germanicus to Rome Tiberius hoped to appease the citizenry and eliminate Germanicus as a rival. The fact that the victories in the European wilderness were exaggerated was kept from the common Roman citizen. More surprising perhaps was Germanicus' willing participation. He of all people knew the truth. His legions had inflicted a measure of defeat upon the Germanic hordes under the command of Arminius but they had in the end only achieved symbolic victory and had not advanced Rome's holdings beyond the traditional boundary of the Rhine and Elbe.

Tradition holds that the conquering hero would ride in a chariot dressed to appear as the Roman god Jupiter. With face painted red and attired in purple robes Germanicus would have rode through the city streets of Rome to the loud acclaim of its citizens. Accompanying Germanicus would have been a slave whose sole purpose was to whisper into the ear of the hero "remember that you are a man. You are not a god." As stated earlier the entire affair was a ruse and was soon perceived as such by an adoring city for only a collection of a few slaves, nearly dead soldiers, and the wife and son of Arminius were on parade. Neither Arminius nor his generals were seen.

One of the clearest distinguishing characteristics of the new atheism is its moral certitude. Richard Dawkins, Christopher Hitchens, and Samuel Harris have declared that atheism has finally and convincingly won the war against Christian theism. So sure are they of this decisive victory that they have made loud proclamation of the fact and proudly published their summaries of the conflict. Dawkins's *The God Delusion,* Hitchens's *God Is Not Great,*

Harris's *The End of Faith,* and Dennett's *Breaking the Spell* all smack of a false triumph similar to that of Germanicus. They fancy themselves as riding in the victor's chariot waving to an adoring crowd.

The new atheists have announced to the world that atheism and science as demonstrated within scientific naturalism has won the day. To commemorate this atheistic victory the new atheists wish to be called "brights."[43] The logic behind the name change appears to be two-fold. The word atheist carries historically negative baggage that must be shed. The second reason is more nuanced. Brights as Dawkins and Daniel Dennett mean the term to be understood represents the conquering of Christian theism and its attendant supernaturalism, mysticism, and metaphysical dimensions through the power of rationalism.

This begs the question of what atheists believed before their name change. Clearly nothing has changed since atheists rejected these Christian theistic categories prior to their evolution to become brights. But have they really rejected the notion of metaphysics? Something more must be afoot here.

Francis Schaeffer was not the first but he certainly was one of the most forceful and influential Christian apologists of the past century. Schaeffer's analysis of the atheistic dilemma speaks to the current situation of the new atheists.

---

[43]D'Souza, 22.

Mankind exists within this universe with a rational knowledge of himself within the physical world and of the cosmos or supernatural realm. Schaeffer refers to this as the upstairs and downstairs of human experience. Atheism by its nature has rejected and thus destroyed the upstairs – cosmos/supernatural – because they believe it cannot be known. It has already been demonstrated that this is an a priori assumption of the atheist not based on evidence. The effect of this division destroys the unity within man and as Schaeffer points out, he becomes divided within himself.

Because man revolted against God and tried to stand autonomous, the great alienation is in the area of man's separation from God. When that happened, then everything else went too. This autonomy is carried over into the very basic area of epistemology, of knowing, so that man is not only divided from other men in the area of knowing, he is divided from himself . . . . He has no universals to cover the particulars in his own life. He is one thing inside and another thing outside. Then he begins to scream, "Who am I?" . . . . It is not just some psychological thing, as we usually think of psychology. It is basically epistemological. Man's attempted autonomy has robbed him of reality. He has nothing to be sure of when his imagination soars beyond the stars, if there is nothing to guarantee a distinction between reality and fantasy. But on the basis of the Christian epistemology, this confusion is ended, the alienation is healed. This is the heart of the problem of knowing, and it is not solved until our knowledge fits under the apex of the infinite-personal, triune God who is there and who is not silent.[44]

Schaeffer points out that only some form of a mystical "jump" can account for the atheist belief that personality comes from impersonality.[45] The same is true for values, morals, and ethics. Dawkins and his peers have attempted to attribute this to what they call the "selfish gene" that in spite of the evolutionary encoding of survival of the fittest operates in an altruistic manner. This twist or slight of hand is what gives Dawkins, Hitchens, and Harris their bravado. They reject the Christian belief in metaphysical reality at the same time they affirm it with different words. The new atheists appeal to a softer, gentler, kinder form of atheism that cannot be reasoned from the tenets undergirding their belief system. They may parade around the book circuit receiving the accolades of the unsuspecting but the fact is they have smuggled Christian theistic transcendence into their atheism.

Dawkins and his peers believe that they can divert attention from the logical and observable devastation of their views by launching a media-blitz of what amounts to nothing more than so much hot air and verbose hubris. The force of Christian theism in relation to the new atheists is best demonstrated by continuing to hold them accountable for the logical outcomes of their views. Barr rightly states that "the inescapable conclusion is that Dawkins and

---

[44]Francis A. Schaeffer, *The God Who Is There,* (Downers Grove, IL: InterVarsity Press, 1968), 83, 341.

[45]Ibid., 95.

materialists of his sort do not in fact stand up full-face into the keen wind of understanding. They don't face the implications of their ideas. If they did, they would have to dismiss all talk of morality, rebellion against nature, and intellectual freedom as so much sentimentality."[46]

Three very distinct and troubling points emerge from the new atheism. First, when God is rejected atheistic humanism fills the void. If there is no infinite, objective reality then man is left with the material universe and its finiteness. Relativism and subjectivism ensue and overwhelm. Malcolm Muggeridge said it best, "If God is dead then someone will have to take his place."[47] Man thus becomes the measure of all things and poetically the captain of his own soul. This is atheism in a nutshell. Second, if God is rejected then mankind must make their bodies their souls. When the eternal is dismissed then space and time is all that remains. Logic and reason are no longer guiding lights instead feelings and emotions ascend to the throne of man's heart. Transcendent ethics that serve to bind man together in community are destroyed and individualism reigns. Into the abyss created by the rejection of the eternal fall such ideals as nobility, justice, law, and liberty, replaced by the arbitrary and iniquitous power of fallen man. Darwinian atheism is most ferocious at this point. Man becomes object and object becomes

---

[46]Barr, 29.

[47]This quote was attributed to Muggeridge by Ravi Zacharias in his teaching "What Happened After God's Funeral" available at www.rzim.org Accessed January 21, 2009. The three points made in conclusion here are from the same teaching although expounded upon for the purposes of this paper.

utilitarian and therefore expendable to the greater good as deemed so by those in positions of power. Third and finally, if God is rejected as He is in atheism mankind is left with space and time as eternity. If life is all there is to a man's existence then he is naïve at best and deceived at worse to enjoin himself to a moral code other than one of his own making. Moral distinctions vanish into a sea of individual relativism culturally and totalitarianism politically. This has been the experience of mankind especially in the twentieth century. The madness and violence wrought by Hitler, Stalin, and Mao accounted for nearly twenty million deaths. They embraced atheism and rejected God as an illusion. This was exactly what Nietzsche saw as the logical conclusion to atheism and he recoiled at the sight.

Contrasting the dire predicament of twenty-first century man, Christian theism offers hope and clear, consistent answers. When God is acknowledged as Creator and Sustainer life becomes infused with meaning and purpose. Man is able to see the beauty and splendor of life and know that he is not alone. Because man has not been left alone he can know that his soul transcends space and time and he is not confused about the material part of existence. Indeed we have the opportunity to understand that the soul of every man is in need of salvation and reconciliation. Only Christian theism speaks of hope beyond the grave. Because God is we can know that salvation has been achieved for us through Jesus Christ.

Christian theism must be not the whisperer but the herald that the new atheism is not new at all and is just as bankrupt as classical atheism. Man is not now nor has he ever been god and it is Christian theism that must continue to remind Dawkins and his peers of this truth.

ABOUT THE AUTHOR

Mike Spaulding has planted two Calvary Chapel churches - Calvary Christian Fellowship, St. Marys, Ohio, in 1998, and Calvary Chapel of Lima, Ohio, in 2005, where he currently serves as pastor.

Mike holds a B.A. in Organizational Management, a M.T.S., and a Ph.D. in apologetics. He is the author of *#MTPGA (Make the Pulpit Great Again): 12 Things Christians Can Do Right Now*, as well as numerous articles including "Leadership and Organizational Vision," "Servant Leadership," and "The Ministry of Teaching" all published by Lifeway Publishers. He is a contributing author to *The Baker Dictionary of World Religions*, H. Wayne House, General Editor. His teaching ministry is featured on the radio program "The Transforming Word," heard on radio stations throughout the Midwest United States.

Mike's past professional memberships included the Evangelical Philosophical Society, The Evangelical Theological Society, and the International Society of Christian Apologetics.

Mike has been married to his lovely wife Kathy for over 35 years and together they have four daughters and five grandchildren.

Made in the USA
Middletown, DE
18 January 2020